TURKISH CULINARY ART

To all current and past students of the Turkish Cooking Classes
in Turquoise Center in Richardson, TX (2009-2013)

17 16 15 14 1 2 3 4

Published by Blue Dome Press

535 Fifth Avenue, Ste. 601

New York, NY 10017-8019

www.bluedomepress.com

Library of Congress Cataloging-in-Publication Data Available

ISBN: 978-1-935295-55-6

Recipes and photographs by

Nevin Gezgin, Emel Yilmaz, Gamze Betul Bulut, Bedile Kara, Reyhan Vural,
Fatma Ziyanak, Beyhan Baydere, Maya Abdygapurova, Emine Ahsen

Edited by Gwen Ellison

Art Director: Engin Çiftçi

Graphic Design: Nurmuhammet Ceyhan

Printed by

Görsel Dizayn Ofset Matbaacılık Tic. Ltd. Şti., Istanbul - Turkey
+90 212 671 91 00

TURKISH CULINARY ART

A Journey through Turkish Cuisine

Gamze B. Bulut, Nevin Gezgin & Emel Yılmaz

RAINDROP FOUNDATION

BLUE DOME

New York

CONTENTS

FOREWORD

Modern day Turkey is, for the most part, the cultural successor of the Ottoman Empire. This empire was a collection of many different nation states, various ethnicities, religions, cultures, and culinary traditions. This great diversity created something more influential, more significant, and more enjoyable; something that many countries treasured and shared until this day known as the Turkish Cuisine. This exceptional environment was unique enough to influence and develop an exquisite fine cuisine that was, and still is, the heart and center of this region.

Historically, Turkish cuisine was influenced by a variety of cultures from the Byzantines, Romans, Persians, Arabs, Balkans and Caucasus to Greeks that lived in the region, and contributed their culinary skills to this extraordinary and remarkable cuisine. This co-mingling of cultures created one of the ultimate feasts in the world. Numerous tasty, colorful dishes and treats that are so delicious, healthy, but yet so simple and easy to prepare.

Some Middle-Eastern and Mediterranean countries share the same names for many dishes that are still a part of the Turkish kitchen, such as hummus, kebabs, baklava, and stuffed grape leaves. Nevertheless, Turkey managed to preserve its own unique signature dishes that are exclusive to Turkey. This great cuisine has been powerful enough to set people's differences aside, and unite them to sit down to enjoy one great meal together, and an aromatic cup of coffee or tea.

Our Cooking classes at the Dallas Turquoise Center have a similar idea of the history of this cuisine introduced centuries ago. People from different backgrounds, ethnicities, and cultures get together to share and enjoy the art of Turkish cooking proudly presented by TAWA volunteers who are there every cooking class helping organize, cook, support, and entertain the audience. They have created the ultimate team to carry on this enjoyable task to spread the Turkish culinary skills to our great cooking class community. The best part of this class is the most exciting minute that audience have been waiting impatiently for where we receive the delicious food and start digging in. We spend hours having conversations, sharing ideas, and discussing important matters of our diverse society, where all of our different cultures meet and live.

Gwen Ellison said, "I have been to Turkey five times, but because of the TAWA cooking class it feels like many more. What a treat it is to take a mini-vacation two Saturday afternoons a month."

Long time member and friend, Melanie Cottam said, "A bouquet of lovely young ladies in beautiful brightly colored silk headscarves have been our teachers at the TAWA Turkish Cooking Class. Intelligent, talented, cheerful and genuinely gracious, these women have taught us cuisines from all regions of Turkey handed down through their families from generation to generation. Geography, history and culture have been woven into the lessons to enhance the experience.

Presentation was learned first hand when they invited us into their homes during Ramadan for Iftar meals, included us in Henna Parties for brides and involved us in cooking competitions at Turkish Festivals in Houston and Richardson.

Homemade yogurt, lemon, garlic, dill, mint, red pepper paste, exotic spices, bulgur, semolina, lentils and special rice are a few of the ingredients that are blended to create delicious dishes. We have also been taught about phyllo, breads and the art of handling the dough. Appetizers, main courses, salads, vegetables and heavenly desserts have all been on the menus. After each class we were served the meal and a glass of Turkish Tea in traditional tulip glasses. The best demonstration was the mixture of different cultures, religions, and generations that resulted in lasting loving friendships. A true recipe for World Peace.

And finally, as one of our regular students and dear friend, Althea Merrick, said, "Great fun! Wonderful people! Terrific food! Warm environment!" and "The ladies who taught the class were lovely, the fragrances tantalizing and the food very good. The stories along the way made for great entertainment. All in all, it was a really fun afternoon! Can't wait for the next class."

Also, we would like to thank all of our friends and members who come to join our cooking class family and share a meal and a cup of tea with us. If it were not for you, we would not be able to write this cooking book. We appreciate your support, attendance and feedback, and we are always delighted to have you back.

A Turkish proverb says, "With a glass of coffee comes of friendship for forty years. "We may not realize this, but sharing a meal has its great mystical power that bonds us together, and I am sure that sharing recipe is even more powerful. Please enjoy these fine, healthy, easy recipes and meals.

Afiyet olsun or bon appétit.

Dalin Sakoglu

THINGS TO KNOW ABOUT TURKEY

Turkey is an eastern Mediterranean country bridging Asia and Europe.

It is the second largest country in Europe, and is a little bigger than the state of Texas. Turkey is a very crowded country, with a population of 75 million on 300,000 square miles.

The official language is Turkish. Turkey is democratic, secular and social state governed by the rule of law; based on the principle of the separation of powers.

Turkey is growing stronger every day with its economy, which is the 17th largest economy in the world.

The Turkish education system has been greatly improved, 12 years of compulsory education and more than 170 universities all around the country. There is no fee for continuing higher education, and successful students receive scholarships from the government.

Turkey has a very rich history. Anatolia was the heart of the Ottoman Empire (1299-1923). The 16th century was the golden age of Ottoman history and culture. The borders of the empire extended from the Crimea in the North, to Yemen and Sudan in the South, and from Iran and the Caspian Sea in the East to Vienna in the Northwest and Spain in the Southwest. After the "War of Independence" the "Republic of Turkey" was founded on October 29, 1923 by Turkish leader Mustafa Kemal Ataturk.

Major cities of Turkey are Istanbul, Ankara, Izmir, Bursa and Konya.

Istanbul, which was once known as Constantinople, has been of special interest to many nations and has been fought over for a long time. The city of Istanbul lies along two sides of the Bosphorus, which makes it very attractive. Here is a photo

of the Bosphorus Bridge and the Levent financial district in the background.

Turkey is the world's largest producer of hard-shell nuts, figs and apricots.

Turkey is the fourth largest producer of fresh vegetables, grape and tobacco; seventh largest of wheat and cotton.

Turkish delight and helva are famous throughout the world.

The most famous and finest pure silk carpets of the world are produced in the small town of Hereke, 60 km east of İstanbul.

Van province of Turkey is famous for its "Van cat" also known as swimming cat, which has two eyes with different colors (one blue, one amber).

Temple of Artemis and the Mausoleum at Halicarnassus, the two of the seven wonders of the ancient world, are in Turkey.

According to legend, Noah's Ark landed on Agri Dagi (Mount Ararat) in Eastern Turkey.

Istanbul's Robert College (established in 1863), is the first American school outside the United States.

Writing was first used by people in ancient Anatolia. The first clay tablets – in the ruins of Assyrian Karum (Merchant Colony – date back to 1950 B.C.)

HISTORICAL AND TOURISTIC PLACES IN TURKEY

TROY

Ancient city of Troy is located 30 km south west of Çanakkale province in the Marmara Region of Turkey. Nine separate periods of settlement: The earliest dates from five thousand years ago (3000 B.C.) and the last coincided with the late Roman period (400 A.D.). Famous Trojan wars – depicted in Homer's epic Iliad – took place here at about 1200 BC. A symbolic wooden horse at this site commemorates this legendary war.

CAPADOCCIA

Cappadocia region is the place where nature and history come together most beautifully within the world. While geographic events are forming Peribacaları (fairy chimneys), during the historical period, humans had carried the signs of thousand years old civilizations with carving houses and churches (underground cities) within these earth pillars and decorating them with frisks.

EPHESUS

The ruins of Ephesus is one of the world's greatest archaeological sites. In Hellenistic times, Ephesus became the most densely populated city in Anatolia with a population of more than 200 000. The city reached the peak of its glory under the Roman rule and became a very important centre of trade and commerce. A majority of the monuments that exist now date to that period.

THE HOUSE OF VIRGIN MARY

This holy site – a modest stone house where the Virgin Mary lived her last days – is in the Bülbül Mountain above Ephesus. It is believed that St. John brought Mary to this site after Christ's Crucifixion; she lived and died here at the age of 101. Vatican declared The House of The Virgin Mary a holy site in 1967.

THE SULTANAHMET MOSQUE

The most famous monument in both the Turkish and the Islamic world. Built in the classic Turkish architectural style between 1609-1616 by the architect Mehmet. Also known as the Blue Mosque because of its magnificent interior paneling of more than 20,000 blue and white İznik tiles.

HAGIA SOPHIA

Hagia Sophia (Ayasofya) was constructed by Roman Emperor Justinian in 537 AD. It was the largest church in the Christian world for a thousand years. The mosaics covering the walls are among the most important works of art that have survived to this day of the Byzantine era.

SOME FAMOUS TURKISH PEOPLE

SULTAN MEHMET THE CONQUEROR

Sultan Mehmet II conquered Byzantine Constantinople (present-day Istanbul) in 1453.

The Sultan was well known for the great tolerance with which he treated his subjects, especially among the conquered Byzantines. He appointed the former Patriarch as essentially governor of the city, and established a *millet* (nation) system which is division of society into communities with each individual or group belonging to one *millet* or another according to religious affiliation... Each millet established and maintained its own institutions to care for the functions not carried out by the ruling class and state, such as education, religion, justice and social security. The Millet system allowed the development and maintenance of ethnic identity on the part of minority subjects within the Ottoman Empire. Greek Orthodox Christians were established as the first major *millet* and the Greek Orthodox patriarchal was recognized within the Millet system.

SULTAN BAYAZID II

Sultan Bayazıd II sent out the Ottoman navy to Spain in 1492 to safely bring Jews, who were fleeing the Spanish Inquisition, to Ottoman lands. Sultan Bayazid II's offer of refuge gave new hope to the persecuted Sephardim. In 1492, the Sultan ordered the governors of the provinces of the Ottoman Empire "not to refuse the Jews' entry or cause them difficulties, but to receive them cordially." According to Bernard Lewis, "the Jews were not just permitted to settle in the Ottoman lands, but were encouraged, assisted and sometimes even compelled."

MAWLANA JALALUDDIN RUMI

Mevlana, who is also known as Rumi, was a philosopher and mystic of Islam.

His doctrine advocates unlimited tolerance, positive reasoning, goodness, charity and awareness through love. To him and to his disciples all religions are more or less truth. Looking with the same eye on Muslim, Jew and Christian alike, his peaceful and tolerant teaching has appealed to men of all sects and creeds.

> Come, come again, whoever you are, come!
>
> Heathen, fire worshipper or idolatrous, come!
>
> Come even if you broke your penitence a hundred times,
>
> Ours is the portal of hope, come as you are.

Rumi was born in 1207 Balkh (present-day Afghanistan) which was then part of the Persian Empire. Rumi spent most of his life living in Turkey and was buried in Konya, Turkey. To celebrate the 800th birth anniversary of Rumi UNESCO has announced that the year 2007 will be the International Year of Rumi. During the year special ceremonies and programs were held over the world to commemorate this great Muslim scholar and poet, particularly in Turkey. Rumi is the best selling poet in the Unites States and in most of the English-speaking world.

YUNUS EMRE

Yunus Emre is one of the most significant folk poet in the history of Islamic literature, besides being the most important Turkish poet up to the twentieth century. His poetry embodies the quintessence of Turkish-Anatolian Islamic humanism and has been a source of inspiration in Turkish intellectual life through the ages. UNESCO named Yunus Emre one of the main cultural figures of world, and dedicated 1991 as "The International Yunus Emre Year." His verses include eloquent specimens of tolerance and universalism:

Sufi is what they call me,
Hate is my only enemy.
I harbour a grudge against none.
To me the whole wide world is one.

Come, let us get to know each other for once
Let us make life easy on us,
Let us be lovers and beloved ones,
The world shall be left to no one.

SOME TURKISH WORDS

Merhaba (Hello)

Güle Güle (Goodbye)

Günaydın (Good morning)

Nasılsın? (How are you?)

Hoşçakal (Bye)

Inşaallah (God willing, I hope)

ABOUT TURKISH CUISINE

Anyone having the pleasure of eating some "stuffed grape leaves" (yaprak sarma) might wonder how this delicate dish came to be. Who could have thought to bring together seemingly unrelated ingredients to form such an exquisite example of Turkish cuisine? Rice, currants, pine nuts, herbs and spices, and grape leaves, are rolled pencil-thin and are cooked together to form a delightful culinary combination. This is only one of the numerous culinary treasures that Turkish cuisine offers.

For anyone considered to be a gourmet, or for anyone interested in the preparation, or the consumption of fine food, Turkish cuisine would rank alongside French, Italian, Chinese and Indian cuisines. Unlike French cuisine with its sauces, or Italian cuisine with its variety of pastas, or Indian cuisine with the different types of curries, it is hard to pinpoint a single leading element in Turkish cooking. The complexity of flavors and the intricate techniques used to create those flavors, the variety of dishes that make up the cuisine, the diversity amongst dishes from various geographical and cultural regions, the way in which all of the different components of a meal come together in a feast-like fashion offer enough material for a life-long study of Turkish cuisine. Even a simple milk pudding will have countless varieties such as "Afyon Sarması" (Afyon Rolls), "Kazandibi" (Caramelized milk pudding) "Keskul" (Almond pudding), "Sutlac" (Rice pudding), and even a variety called "Tavuk Gogsu" (Chicken Breast Pudding).

The Turkish state of Anatolia is around 1,000 years old, so the development of such a complex cuisine is not an accident. For a millennium, Turks have set on the crossroads of culture and trade, as the Silk Road has ran through the heart of the Turkish civilization since the Turks made their way into Anatolia in 1071 CE. The Silk Road brought with it an abundance of wealth and culture, which shaped the growth of Turkish cuisine. Alongside the Silk Road, the stability present in the Anatolian region, in the form of long-standing empires, has also contributed heavily to the development of Turkish cuisine. Both the Seljuk Empire and the Ottoman Empire had imperial kitchens where hundreds of cooks all specialized in a variety of different dishes and techniques. The cultural transitions from the Seljuk Empire to the Ottoman Empire, and the Ottoman Empire to the modern Turkish Republic were not traumatic, so there was no discontinuation of the great culinary traditions. A final condition essential to the development of such a rich cuisine is the diversity of the flora and fauna present in Anatolia. Geographically speaking, Anatolia is a small, but incredibly diverse region. The weather varies so drastically from the North to the South, and from the East to the West that there is an incredible abundance of ingredients. Each geographical region in Turkey makes full use of the ingredients, the landscape and weather in producing phenomenally different flavors. The "Kara Lahana Sarma" (Stuffed collard greens) of the Black Sea region is very different from the "Yaprak Sarma" (Stuffed grape leaves) of the Aegean region, which is very different from the "Beyaz Lahana Sarma" (Stuffed white cabbage) of the Central Anatolian region. While these dishes are all based on the same technique – wrapping, rice and a combination of ingredients in different leafy vegetables – the tastes and textures formed are vastly different.

These characteristics and the unique cultural and historical traditions of the Turkish people have given Turkish cuisine a very rich collection of dishes. These dishes will all be prepared in different ways, using different ingredients, and will be combined with different dishes to create an infinite variety of meals depending on which regional style is being observed. Our goal with this book is to help those interested in Turkish food experience some of these flavor combinations in the comfort of their own homes. We will try to simplify some of the complex techniques required in preparing these dishes without disrespecting the long tradition associated with each dish, or compromising the quality of any dish.

Please enjoy your journey through Turkey's culinary treasures. Afiyet olsun.

CONVERSION CHART

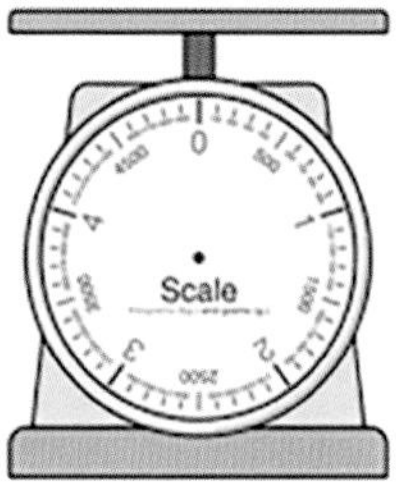

Volume		
1 US tablespoon	=	3 US teaspoons
1 US fluid ounce	≅	29.57 milliliters (ml)
1 US cup	=	16 US tablespoons
1 US cup	=	8 US fluid ounces
1 US pint	=	2 US cups
1 US pint	=	16 US fluid ounces
1 liter (l)	≅	33.81 US fluid ounces
1 liter (l)	=	1000 milliliters (ml)
1 US quart	=	2 US pints
1 US gallon	=	4 US quarts
1 US gallon	=	3.78 liters

Weight		
1 milligram (mg)	=	0.001 grams (g)
1 gram (g)	=	0.001 kilograms (kg)
1 gram (g)	≅	0.035 ounces
1 ounce	=	28.35 grams (g)
1 ounce	=	0.0625 pounds
1 pound (lb)	=	16 ounces
1 pound (lb)	=	0.45 kilograms (kg)
1 kilogram (kg)	=	1000 grams
1 kilogram (kg)	≅	35.27 ounces
1 kilogram (kg)	≅	2.20 pounds (lb)

Temperature	
Celsius °C	Fahrenheit °F
18 °C	64.4 °F
19 °C	66.2 °F
20 °C	68.0 °F
21 °C	69.8 °F
22 °C	71.6 °F
23 °C	73.4 °F
24 °C	75.2 °F
25 °C	77.0 °F
26 °C	78.8 °F
27 °C	80.6 °F
28 °C	82.4 °F
29 °C	84.2 °F
30 °C	86.0 °F
40 °C	104 °F
50 °C	122 °F
60 °C	140 °F

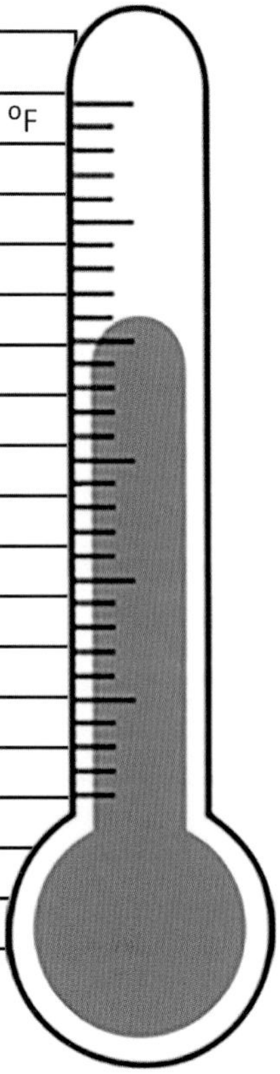

FIGURE LEGEND

Each star show the hardness of each recipe. Inside the document, it is indicated with number of stars next to the name of the dish.

1 star = easiest

...

5 stars = hardest

* (easy)

**(easy-medium)

***(medium)

****(medium-hard)

*****(hard)

KITCHEN TRICKS

1. To keep mushrooms from discoloring before cooking, soak them for about 10 minutes in water to cover with 1 tbsp lemon juice added right before cooking.
2. To keep peeled potatoes from discoloring, cover in salted water. Rinse before using.
3. If you want your rice to be really white, add 3 drops lemon juice or ½ tsp sugar to the cooking water.
4. To correct overseasoning, you can add pinch of sugar to a salty dish or a pinch of salt to a sweet dish.
5. To eliminate refrigerator odor, put 1 cotton ball and 1 tbsp baking soda in a small cup in your refrigerator, changing every 3 weeks.
6. Add bay leaf on the fish while baking fish to absorb the fish smell.
7. To peel tomatoes more easily, first drop in boiling water for a minute.
8. The skins of recently boiled potatoes and roasted eggplants will be easier to remove if they are carefully placed in a plastic freezer bag while they are still hot and left to steam for about 15 minutes.
9. Sliced eggplants can be soaked in salted water to eliminate any bitter taste.
10. To easily slice bread, use a warm knife.
11. To keep cut fruit from discoloring, cover in water that includes the juice of half a lemon.
12. While boiling potatoes, add ½cup milk to the water to make them tastier.
13. To clean your sinks and countertops, make a mixture of 1 quart water and 2 tbsp baking soda and wipe with a cloth.
14. Reserve water used to boil eggs. Once cool, use it to water your plants. This water is rich in calcium and minerals. Your plants will love it.
15. To peel boiled eggs more easily, add a pinch of salt to the boiling water.
16. You can use the cut surface of a lemon to polish any stainless steel utensil. That includes appliances like fridge, dish washer, oven which would be hard to wash) in your kitchen. Wash thoroughly afterwards.
17. If you don't want your eyes to be irritated when cutting onions, soak the onions in water for couple of minutes first.
18. Soak beans overnight in warm water with 1-2 tbsp baking soda added. They will cook more easily and cooking time will shorten by 10 minutes.
19. While preparing béchamel sauce, add the salt after the sauce thickens to avoid curdling the milk.
20. To keep salt flowing freely, add a few grains of raw rice to the shaker.
21. If while cooking a broth you realize is too salty, add few potato cubes. They will absorb the extra salt. Discard them when no longer needed.
22. If the eggs you use in cake are at room temperature, your cake will rise better and easier.

23. Lemon juice tenderizes meat. If you add 1 tsp lemon juice for every pound of meat while cooking), it will cook sooner and be more tender and delicious.

24. If a lemon is hard and doesn't seem juicy, warm in hot water before cutting.

25. If you don't want the food you bake to dry out in the oven, put one cup of water in an oven safe container next to your dish to provide steam while baking.

26. To clean burned-on food from pots and pans, spread baking soda to cover the burned part and add water to a 1 inch depth. Bring to a boil and simmer for 5 minutes. Scrub and repeat the process if needed.

27. Always temper yogurt and raw egg yolk with a bit of hot liquid before adding to a boiling soup.

28. Never mix egg whites into soup. Egg whites will cook and make lumps. Using just the yolk of an egg makes a much smoother soup.

29. Never add hot water to a cooked butter and flour mixture, it will make lumps. Add cold water instead.

30. For more attractive deviled eggs, turn each egg upside down in the carton the night before cooking them. This re-centers the yolks that have settled since the eggs were packaged.

SAMPLE MENUS

1. Iskender Kebab, Vegetable Soup, Bean Salad and Sobiyet dessert.
2. Black eyed pea and noodle soup (Unash), Turkmen Pilaf, Mimosa Salad (with fish), Ant Hill Cookies.
3. Cokertme Kebab, Broccoli Soup, Olive bread and Noah's Pudding (Ashure).
4. Talas Pastry, Roasted Veggies, Potato patties, mole dessert.
5. Chicken Soup, Hasan Pasha Kofte, Bulghur pilaf with green lentils and riddled cookies.
6. Ali Nazik Kebab, Rice Pilaf, Season Salad and Butternut squash dessert.
7. Circassian Chicken, potato salad, flat bread with spinach and cookies with marmalade.
8. Muradiye Soup, Plum Stew, Purslane salad and Semolina halvah with ice cream.
9. Zucchini gratin, leeks and carrots, cheese pastry with oregano, cyprus dessert.
10. Lamb kebab, bulghur pilaf, fried cauliflower, apple cookies.
11. Collard greens soup, chicken kapama, green beans, gullac dessert.
12. Meatball soup, walnut rolls, zucchini fritters, tahini cake.
13. Mushroom soup, clay pot lamb and veggies, orzo pilaf, kadaif with pudding.
14. Stuffed collard greens, tomato soup with vermicelli, rolled phyllos with chicken, sambali dessert.
15. Izmir meatballs, pastry with spinach and feta cheese, green lentils salad, carrot cake.
16. Islim kebab, couscous pilaf, season salad, cinnamon tahini cookies.
17. Stuffed bell peppers, crunchy potato pastries, circassian chicken, walnut cookies.
18. Tarhana soup, tantuni kebab, onion tomato salad, riddled cookies.
19. Stuffed eggplants, cheese pastry, mushroom salad, custard with chocolate sauce.
20. Sheet pastry with leeks, wedding soup, yogurt drink, tiramisu.
21. Meatball stew, stuffed grape leaves, carrot zucchini salad, almond pudding.
22. Ezogelin soup, lamb kebab, orzo salad, kataifi dessert.
23. Chicken with peas, bulghur pilaf, shepherd's salad, mosaic cake with tea biscuits.
24. Dry beans with sausage, rice pilaf, yogurt with cucumbers, apple tea biscuit dessert.
25. Meatballs with rice, cheese pastries, mashed potato, toasted bread dessert.
26. Turkish pizza (lahmacun), tomato cucumber salad, stuffed grape leaves, shekerpare.
27. Clay pot lamb with vegetables, rice pilaf with tomatoes, bean salad, Noah's pudding.

28. Fried ravioli, green lentil soup with noodles, purple salad, rice pudding.
29. Chicken shish kebab, chi-kofte, tomato dip, kunefe dessert.
30. Fried anchovies, black sea region flatbread with cheese (pide), green salad, butternut squash dessert.
31. Stuffed zucchinis, yogurt, vegetarian fellah balls, semolina halvah.
32. Winter Salad, Rice with Almonds, Baked Trout fish, Rolled Baklava
33. Forest Kebab, Bosnian Pastry with spinach, Garden salad with Yogurt and sour cream, and White mosaic tea biscuit dessert.
34. Lentil patties, pacanga pastry, menemen, baklava
35. Fine bulghur salad, beyti kebab with lavash bread, shekerpare.
36. Flat bread with cheese, lentil patties, cyprus pilaf, wet cake with figs.
37. Azerbaijani dumpling soup, chicken salad, fresh herb omelet, zebra cake.
38. Boat delight (stuffed eggplants), bulghur pilaf, green salad, apricot and raisin compote.

SOUPS

Serving of Turkish Dinner

Turkish dinners usually start with a bowl of soup. This helps the digestive system become ready for the food to be eaten later. Drinking soup before meal is also helpful for weight maintenance by filling the stomach. Next, main dish is served along with side dishes (such as rice pilaf, salads and pastries). Finally, dessert is served usually with tea or coffee.

Tempering the Soup

Soups made with yogurt generally require tempering the yogurt mixture in the soup. The purpose of tempering yogurt is to increase the temperature of yogurt gradually so that it will not curdle when mixed in the soup. To temper your yogurt slowly add about half cup of the soup mixture at a time and mix thoroughly.

TOMATO SOUP WITH VERMICELLI (SEHRIYELI DOMATES CORBASI)*

INGREDIENTS

3 tomatoes (peeled)

2 tbsp butter

4 c water

½ c vermicelli noodles

Salt to taste

Parsley

PREPARATION

Puree tomatoes. Melt the butter in a saucepan, add the tomatoes, and cook over medium heat for 5 minutes, stirring occasionally. Add water and bring to a boil before adding the vermicelli and salt. Boil the soup until the vermicelli is soft. Garnish with finely chopped parsley.

RED LENTIL SOUP (MERCIMEK CORBASI)**

INGREDIENTS

1 small onion (chopped)

1 c red lentils (rinsed and drained)

4 tbsp butter

2 tbsp flour

Salt to taste

Lemon wedges (on the side)

PREPARATION

Mix onion and lentils in a pot. Add water to cover, bring to a boil and cook until lentils are soft, about 15-20 minutes. Cool until it's safe to puree the mixture. If you used a blender or food processor, return the mixture to the pan. Bring to a boil over medium-high heat. In a small pan, cook melted butter and flour on medium-low heat until it starts turning brown, being careful not to burn it. Whisk into the boiling soup and cook until thickened. Add salt and serve with lemon wedges.

YOGURT SOUP (YOGURT CORBASI)**

INGREDIENTS

¼ c rice

5 c water (if you wish you can use half chicken stock, half water)

1 c plain yogurt

3 egg yolks

2 tbsp flour

3 tbsp butter (divided use)

2 tsp dried mint

Salt to taste

PREPARATION

Boil rice in water until soft, about 10-15 minutes. In a small pan, mix 2 tbsp butter and flour and cook for one minute. Slowly whisk it into the water and rice and boil for 10 minutes. Beat egg yolks and yogurt and temper with 2 tbsp of the soup mixture. Add the yogurt and egg mixture to the soup and cook on very low heat (so that the yogurt doesn't curdle) for 2-3 minutes, stirring constantly. Melt 1 tbsp butter in a pan. Once it sizzles, add mint flakes and stir constantly for 20-30 seconds before mixing it into the soup. Add salt after turning the heat off.

CHICKEN SOUP (TAVUK CORBASI)**

INGREDIENTS

1 chicken breast

4 c water

2 tbsp butter

1 tbsp flour

1 c yogurt

1 egg yolk

2 cloves of garlic (minced)

Salt, black pepper, crushed red pepper to taste

PREPARATION

Poach chicken in water. Remove chicken breast from broth and set aside to cool before shredding, reserving broth. In a large saucepan, melt butter and mix in flour, cooking for 1 minute. Whisk in chicken broth, bringing to a boil before adding shredded chicken. In a small bowl, beat yogurt and egg yolk. Temper the mixture with 4 tbsp soup and then whisk into broth, cooking over low heat so that the yogurt does not curdle. Add minced garlic and cook for 5 more minutes. Right before serving, season to taste with, salt, black pepper, and crushed red pepper.

MUSHROOM SOUP (MANTAR CORBASI)**

INGREDIENTS

1 lb mushrooms

1 medium onion (chopped)

2 tbsp butter

2 tbsp flour

4 c hot water

Salt to taste

1½ c milk

Black pepper (freshly ground)

PREPARATION

Clean the mushrooms and chop into small pieces. In a medium pan, sauté onions and mushrooms with butter. Add flour and saute 5 more minutes. Stir in water, milk, and salt and continue cooking for about 20 minutes. Remove from heat. Garnish with black pepper.

EZOGELIN SOUP (EZOGELIN CORBASI)***

PREPARATION

INGREDIENTS

2 tbsp red lentils

2 tbsp rice

2 tbsp fine bulghur (Size #2)

Warm water to cover

Sauce:

1 onion (chopped)

4 tbsp butter

2 tbsp flour

1 tbsp tomato paste

1 tbsp pepper paste

4 c water

2 tbsp vermicelli

Salt, pepper, dried mint to taste

Lemon wedges (on the side)

Place red lentils, rice and bulghur in a large pot and add warm water. Boil until the grains are soft, for about 25 minutes. Meanwhile, saute the onion in oil for 5 minutes over medium heat or until the onion is translucent. Then add flour and cook for one minute, stirring constantly. Stir in tomato paste, pepper paste, mint and other spices. Add 4 cups of water into a pan along with the vermicelli and cooked grains. Stir sauteed onion and spices in to the grains. You can add more water to thin if you wish. Bring to a boil and turn the heat off. Serve with lemon wedges

The story of Ezo,The Bride

Once upon a time there was an exceptionally beautiful woman named "Ezo-gelin" who lived in the province Gaziantep in southeastern Turkey. Ezo had red cheeks and black hair. Travelers passing through her village admired her. It was time for Ezo to find a good match and get married. Unfortunately, she was very unlucky in love. Her first husband was actually in love with another lady and so they divorced. With her second marriage she moved to Syria, but she had a terrible mother-in-law and was very homesick. She had a very unhappy life with many hardships and she got tuberculosis, and stayed in the hospital. She refused to eat hospital food and she made the soup for herself in the hospital. The smell of the soup spread all over the hospital and the soup became famous with her name "ezo gelin." She died of tuberculosis in the 1950s but is still remembered through this recipe and in popular films and folk songs.

POTATO SOUP (PATATES CORBASI)**

INGREDIENTS

1 large onion

4 tbsp butter

4 large potatoes (peeled and cut in ½ inch cubes)

6 c chicken broth

Salt and pepper to taste

Lettuce, finely chopped

PREPARATION

Sauté onions with butter, add potatoes, and continue to sauté for 5 minutes. Add broth, bring to a boil, and then lower heat to simmer. Cook until the potatoes are tender, about 20 minutes. Add salt and pepper. Puree and serve with finely chopped lettuce.

BROCCOLI SOUP (BROKOLI CORBASI)**

INGREDIENTS

1½ lb broccoli

1 onion (chopped)

1 tbsp butter

2 tbsp flour

6 c water

1 c heavy whipping cream

Salt and pepper to taste

PREPARATION

Wash broccoli and separate into florets. Sauté onion in oil about 5 minutes until it is light brown. Add flour to the pan and stir for 2-3 minutes. Whisk in water. When water starts to boil, add broccoli. Cover and reduce heat to a simmer. When broccoli is tender, cool and puree the soup. Stir in cream. Then add salt and black pepper. Bring the soup back to a boil and boil for 5 minutes, stirring constantly. Serve hot.

TARHANA*****

INGREDIENTS

Tarhana:

2 red bell peppers (seeded and cut in chunks)

2 medium onions (roughly chopped)

2 large tomatoes (diced)

¼ tsp yeast, melted in a little bit of warm water

1¾ c yogurt (plain)

1 tbsp dry mint

1 tbsp dry oregano

2 tbsp olive oil

1 tbsp salt

7-8 c flour (the amount of flour can be changed depending on the size of vegetables, add little by little)

PREPARATION OF TARHANA

Boil red pepper and onion until tender, drain. Puree tomato, cooked red peppers and onions. Place in a large bowl with the melted yeast, yogurt, mint, oregano, dill, olive oil and salt. Stir in 2 c of flour and gradually knead in more until you have a thick dough, sprinkling with a little water as needed during the process. Cover the dough with plastic wrap. Leave it at room temperature to ferment 5-6 days. Knead the dough every day for about 4-5 minutes, re-covering with the plastic wrap every time. (Your kitchen might smell a bit sour at this time which is normal.)

The dough is fully fermented when it no longer puffs up. Divide the dough into 4 balls and freeze in plastic bags. If you prefer to dry the dough, divide it into small balls, place the pieces on a cloth and let them dry by turning the balls often. Every day divide each ball into 2 or 3 pieces. It takes a few days. Then either crumble or use a chopper to grind the dried tarhana as much as possible. Store in an airtight container in the fridge.

TARHANA SOUP (TARHANA CORBASI)*

INGREDIENTS

2-3 tbsp tarhana dough crumbles, dried (see above)

2 ½ c water (divided use)

Salt to taste

½ tsp crushed red pepper

2 tbsp butter

PREPARATION

Soften tarhana in ½ cup of water for 2-3 hours. Add softened tarhana and the rest of the ingredients to a saucepan. Cook and stir constantly over medium-low heat. Adjust consistency of the soup by adding more water if you prefer. Taste for salt. Sauté crushed red pepper in butter and top soup with it. Tarhana soup is great for breakfast on cold winter days. Alternatively, you may sauté the dried tarhana in butter for 3-4 minutes. Then stir in water and bring to a boil. Add salt and red pepper to your taste and turn the heat off.

The story of Tarhana

Tarhana is an instant soup mix prepared by Anatolian Turks. The ingredients of Tarhana may include fresh vegetables, yogurt, spices, wheat or corn flour, and chickpeas. Some people eat tarhana in granola bars; some people make soup with it. The story of Tarhana goes like this: Once upon a time, an Ottoman Sultan was visiting a poor family's house (Ottoman Sultans arrange visits to the community occasionally to talk to them and observe their lives first hand). The poor man's wife had only one thing to offer to their important guest. She boiled the Tarhana soup quickly and was embarrassed when serving the soup, but the Sultan said the soup was delicious and asked the name. She said: "This is Dar-hane soup (Poor house soup)." That is why it is called "Tarhana soup" today. (Modified from Binnur's Cookbook)

MURADIYE SOUP (MURADIYE CORBASI)**

INGREDIENTS

4 oz chicken breast (diced)

3 tbsp butter

1 carrot (cut in ½" cubes)

1 zucchini (cut in ½" cubes)

¼ c yogurt

2 tbsp flour

4 c chicken broth

2 tbsp orzo

Salt and pepper to taste

PREPARATION

Brown chicken in a pot with butter. Add carrot, zucchini and continue cooking for 5 minutes. Add chicken broth and bring it to a boil. Add orzo and cook for about 10 minutes, reduce heat to simmer. In a bowl, mix yogurt and flour; temper and stir in yogurt mix to the soup and boil 5 more minutes on low heat. Season with salt and pepper before serving.

COLLARD GREENS SOUP (KARALAHANA CORBASI)***

INGREDIENTS

2 c navy beans (soaked overnight)

8 c water

2 bunches collard greens, finely chopped

3 c corn (canned)

1 tbsp butter

1 tbsp corn or olive oil

Salt to taste

1 c corn flour

PREPARATION

Soak haricot beans overnight. Before cooking, drain and rinse the beans. Bring 8 cups of fresh water to a boil in a large saucepan. Add the beans and cook for 30-40 minutes until softened. Add collard greens, corn, oil, butter and salt. When it returns to a boil, whisk in corn flour slowly. Reduce heat to slow and keep boiling for 10 more minutes before serving.

MEATBALL SOUP (CILLI KOFTE)****

INGREDIENTS

1 lb. ground beef

½ c rice (rinsed and drained)

1 small onion (chopped)

1 egg, divided use

Salt and pepper to taste

1 c flour

4 c water

½ tsp salt

2 carrots (cut in ½" cubes)

2 medium potatoes (cut in ½" cubes)

Juice of ½ lemon

1 tbsp butter

1/2 tsp dried mint

PREPARATION

Mix together ground beef, rice, onion, egg white, salt and pepper and form into marble size balls. Sprinkle flour on a tray and roll meatballs in the flour so they will not stick to one another. In a large pot bring water to a boil and add ½ tsp salt. Add in carrots and boil for 10 minutes. Then stir in potatoes and shake excess flour from meatballs and add to the pot and cook for 15 minutes. Boil the soup until the rice in the meatballs has expanded. In a small bowl, whisk lemon juice and egg yolk. Temper this mixture with 2 tbsp soup liquid before adding to the soup and boiling 2 more minutes. Heat butter in a pan. Once it sizzles, add mint flakes and stir constantly for 20-30 seconds before mixing it into the soup.

WEDDING SOUP (DUGUN CORBASI)****

INGREDIENTS

1 lamb neck

10 c water

1 large onion, quartered

1 medium carrot (cut into ¾" cubes)

Salt to taste

4 tbsp butter

3 tbsp of flour

3 egg yolks

2 tbsp lemon juice

***Garnish*:**

4 tbsp butter

2 teaspoons paprika

1 dash ground red pepper

PREPARATION

Put lamb, water, onion, and carrot in a large stew pot. Bring to a boil and lower heat. Skimming soup frequently, simmer over very low heat for 3 to 4 hours, or until meat falls off the bone. Cool and remove the fat when it sets. Strain the broth. Cut the meat from bones and trim off all fat. Shred the meat and set aside. Discard bones, onion and carrot. Melt butter in the stew pot; stir in flour and brown lightly. Whisk in the broth and cook, stirring constantly, until soup thickens slightly. Beat egg yolks and lemon juice together, temper with ½ c hot soup, and stir into soup. Add shredded meat and salt and heat through without boiling. Meanwhile, for garnish, in a small pan melt butter, add paprika and a dash of ground red pepper. Once it sizzles serve soup immediately with this garnish. Wedding soup is best served with crisp bread sticks or crackers.

GREEN LENTIL SOUP WITH NOODLES (ERISTELI YESIL MERCIMEK CORBASI)**

INGREDIENTS

1 c green lentils

4 c water

½ tsp salt

3 tbsp butter

1 onion (chopped)

1 tbsp tomato paste

½ c noodles

2 tsp salt

2 tsp dried mint

PREPARATION

Rinse and drain lentils, boil in salted water for 10 minutes, and drain. Sauté onions in butter and add tomato paste. Add lentils and 4 cups water. Cooking liquid went down the drain and bring to a boil over medium heat. Add noodles, salt and dried mint, boil for 10 minutes. If the soup gets too thick, thin with hot water.

VEGETABLE SOUP (SEBZE CORBASI)**

PREPARATION

Sauté chopped onion in oil for about 4 minutes. Then, mix in flour and tomato paste and sauté for 2 minutes. Add vegetables and continue sautéing for 2 more minutes. Then add water, salt, pepper, red pepper flakes, lemon juice, bring to a boil and simmer for 50 minutes.

INGREDIENTS

5 tbsp corn oil

1 c onion (chopped)

2 tbsp flour

2 tbsp tomato paste

½ c artichoke (chopped)

2 c cabbage (chopped)

1 c broccoli (chopped)

1 c cauliflower (chopped)

½ c potato (chopped)

1 carrot (chopped)

6 c water

Salt and pepper to taste

¼ tsp red pepper flakes

2 tbsp lemon juice

MAIN DISHES

Tomato / Red Pepper Paste

Tomato and peppers are made into paste to capture the peak of their flavor in the summer for use throughout the year. Tomato and pepper paste are traditionally sun dried to remove most of the moisture. You may purchase tomato paste in your grocery store and red pepper paste in Mediterranean and international stores. Tomato paste can be used in addition to tomatoes in most of the recipes. You may also make tomato juice by diluting tomato paste.

STUFFED EGGPLANTS (KARNIYARIK)***

INGREDIENTS

4 eggplants (Japanese, 7-8 ounces each)

½ cup vegetable oil

½ lb ground beef

1 large onion, diced

2 cloves garlic, minced

2 tomatoes, one sliced thinly, the other one grated

1 tbsp tomato paste (divided use)

Salt and pepper to taste

2 green bell peppers, julienned

½ c boiling water

Parsley, to garnish

PREPARATION

Peel eggplants lengthwise so they appear striped. Place in a large bowl of salted water, top with an inverted plate to keep them submerged and set aside for 30 minutes to remove any bitterness. Drain eggplants and blot excess water with paper towels. Cut into the eggplants lengthwise, being careful to slice just over halfway through. Add the oil to a large skillet and heat over medium-high heat, frying the whole eggplants in two batches until golden brown on all sides, about 5 minutes total. Transfer immediately to a plate lined with paper towel to drain excess oil. Once drained, place eggplants in an 8″x8″ baking dish and set aside. (Alternatively, you may brush eggplants with oil and put under the broiler until softened turning occasionally.)Preheat oven to 375° F.

In a separate skillet, cook ground beef with onion and garlic over medium-high heat until no pink remains. Grate one tomato over the beef mixture. Add ½ tbsp tomato paste, season to taste with salt and pepper and cook until all tomato juices evaporates.

With a small spoon, press the center of the eggplants to open them and then stuff with the ground beef mixture. Slice one tomato thinly and arrange one slice and julienned of green pepper on each eggplant. Whisk boiling water and the remaining tomato paste. Spoon a little over the eggplants to moisten them and pour the rest around them. Bake until the peppers have softened, about 30-40 minutes. Serve warm.

HASAN PASHA MEATBALLS (HASAN PASA KOFTE)****

INGREDIENTS

Mashed Potato ingredients:

5-6 potatoes

1 egg

2 tbsp butter

½ c milk

Salt

Kofte ingredients:

1½ lb ground beef

1 onion (finely diced)

1 tbsp tomato paste

3 tbsp oil

1 egg

½ c bread crumbs

Salt and pepper to taste

Crushed red pepper flakes

Tomato sauce ingredients:

2 tbsp oil

3 tbsp tomato paste

1 c water

PREPARATION

Preheat oven to 350°F. Peel potatoes and boil them. Drain and return to hot saucepan to dry for a couple of minutes. Mash with raw egg, butter, milk, and salt.

Mix kofte ingredients together. Make egg sized balls, poking a hole in the middle of each with your finger. Place kofte, open side up, in an oiled 9"x13" pan and bake for 15-20 minutes. Set aside.

Mix oil with tomato paste. Add water and boil for 2 min. Stuff kofte with potato puree using a teaspoon. Pour the tomato sauce over the top and return to the oven for 10 minutes.

THE STORY OF HASAN PASHA MEATBALLS

Once upon a time, there was a governor named Hasan Pasha in the province of Zigetvar. One day he was walking in the slave market to get some slaves for his mansion. There was a skinny girl with blue eyes named 'Anatolia' among those he chose. Anatolia was a very hardworking woman, and soon she became a leader in the mansion's kitchen. One day there was a big feast to be organized, and they asked Anatolia to cook a special dish. She made this recipe to serve the guests. When served, Hasan Pasha enjoyed the meatballs and asked the name of the dish. They called Anatolia to ask her, and she replied with her respect , "The creation of Anatolia reflecting her love, it is called Hasan Pasha meatballs."

ISLIM KEBAB (ISLIM KEBABI)****

INGREDIENTS

4-5 eggplants (Japanese, 7-8 ounces each)

3-4 tbsp olive oil (to fry eggplants)

Meatball Ingredients:

1 lb ground beef

1 egg

1 onion

1 clove garlic

½ c bread crumbs

Salt and pepper to taste

1 bunch of parsley

⅓ c olive oil (to fry the meatballs)

4-5 Anaheim peppers (sliced lengthwise into strips)

3-4 tomatoes (sliced)

PREPARATION

Preheat oven to 350°F. Peel eggplants lengthwise so they appear striped. Cut the ends and slice eggplants lengthwise into ⅛″ thick pieces. Then fry them in oil for 1-2 minutes per side until golden brown. Remove with a slotted spoon and drain on paper towels while they cool. In a bowl, combine all meatball ingredients and knead till the mixture gets thick for about 5 minutes. Form into plum size balls. Brown the meatballs in olive oil in a fresh sauce pan. Place one eggplant slice horizontally and another vertically in a '+' shape and place one meatball in the middle. Fold over the slices to enclose the meatball and place eggplant package seam side down, on a greased 9″x13″ Pyrex baking dish. Lay a slice of tomato and a slice of green pepper on top and secure with a toothpick. Bake 25-30 minutes.

ISKENDER KEBAB (ISKENDER KEBABI)****

INGREDIENTS

3 c pita bread (cut in 1" squares)

1 lb steak fillet (frozen)

1 tsp salt

¼ c oil (divided use)

1 c water

3 c yogurt

4 tbsp butter

Tomato Sauce:

3 tbsp tomato paste

1 c water

1 tsp salt

1 tsp red pepper flakes

1 tsp black pepper

1 tsp dried oregano

PREPARATION

Preheat oven to 350°F. Take out steak from the freezer 10 minutes before cooking and cut into very thin slices. Put the slices on a baking pan, pour 1 cup water and half of the oil on top and bake in the oven, turning once during baking. When meat broth evaporates, stir in the other half of the oil, lower the heat to 250°F, and bake for 15-20 minutes more. Meanwhile, mix all ingredients for the tomato sauce in a saucepan. Boil for 6-7 minutes and turn off the heat. In a different pot, melt the butter, boiling until the water bubbles out and evaporates and a foam forms on top of the melted butter and set aside. Broil the meat for 3-4 minutes before serving. Place pita bread pieces on a serving dish and pour on half of the tomato sauce. Top with meat and the rest of the tomato sauce. Finally, pour butter over it all and serve with yogurt on the side.

About Doner Kebap

Doner kebab is a Turkish dish made of meat cooked on a vertical spit. Although there is a type of doner made with chicken, the original version is made with a mixture of beef and lamb and special spices. Doner Kebap is also widely known by its Arabic name, shawarma or, as in the United States, by its Greek name gyro.

Doner Kebap in the shape of an inverted cone is cooked by rotating slowly on a vertical rotisserie. Then, for serving it is sliced vertically into thin, crisp shavings. Traditional toppings include tomato, onion, lettuce, green pepper and parsley. The sliced meat of a Doner Kebab is served in three different ways: on a plate, in a wrap, or as a sandwich. It is a common fast food in the Balkans, Middle East, Europe, Australia, and New Zealand. Iskender Kebab is a special kind of Doner which is served over pita bread with tomato sauce, yogurt sauce, and melted butter.

FOREST KEBAB (ORMAN KEBABI)***

INGREDIENTS

2 c corn oil

3 potatoes (peeled and cut in ¾" cubes)

3 zucchinis (peeled and cut in ¾" cubes)

3 eggplants (peeled in stripes and cut in ¾" cubes)

3 green bell peppers (cut in ¾" cubes)

Meatball:

1 lb ground beef

1 onion (grated)

2 garlic cloves (grated)

1 c bread crumbs

3 tbsp olive oil

Salt and pepper to taste

1 bunch of parsley (chopped)

6 tomatoes (grated)

5-6 garlic cloves (chopped)

PREPARATION

Preheat oven to 400°F. Heat corn oil in a pot and deep fry potatoes. Drain them on paper towels and then follow with zucchini, then eggplant, and finally bell pepper. Reserve the oil for the meatballs. In another bowl, mix all meatball ingredients thoroughly, and make grape sized meatballs. Then fry meatballs too. Put fried vegetables in a baking dish. Top with fried meatballs and grated tomato and garlic. Bake for 10 minutes.

COKERTME KEBAB (COKERTME KEBABI)***

INGREDIENTS

1 lb fillet of beef

¼ c olive oil

Salt and pepper to taste

½ tsp chili powder

1 tsp oregano

5-6 potatoes, 2 ½ - 3 lb)

2 cuo olive oil (for frying)

2 c strained plain yogurt

2 cloves garlic (minced)

Salt to taste

Red pepper flakes (optional for garnish)

PREPARATION

Cut the meat diagonally against the grain into strips and brown over medium-high heat in a dry pan. Then add olive oil and stir. Add some water if needed and cook until meat is tender. Add salt, pepper, chili powder, and oregano. Peel potatoes and slice into thin matchsticks (⅛" thick), rinse to remove the starch. Until the starch is gone and Drain and blot dry with paper towels. Fry in oil until golden brown, draining on fresh paper towels. In a bowl mix yogurt, garlic and salt together. Place on a serving plate in this order; fried potatoes, meat and then yogurt mixture. Garnish with red pepper flakes.

MEATBALL PATTIES (KURU KOFTE)**

INGREDIENTS

1 lb ground beef (80%-85% lean)

½ lb ground lamb

1 c bread crumbs

1 medium onion (chopped or shredded)

1 egg

¼ tsp baking soda

½ tsp black pepper

1 tsp cumin

1 tsp oregano

1 tsp salt

PREPARATION

Place all ingredients in a large bowl and mix with your hands for about 15 minutes. Do not worry about over mixing. Wash hands and then grease them with olive oil. Make egg-sized oblong meatballs from the mixture and flatten with the palms of your hands. Heat ¼ cup olive oil in a cast iron frying pan. Fry on both sides and serve hot.

LAVASH BREAD WITH GROUND BEEF (BEYTI KEBAB)**

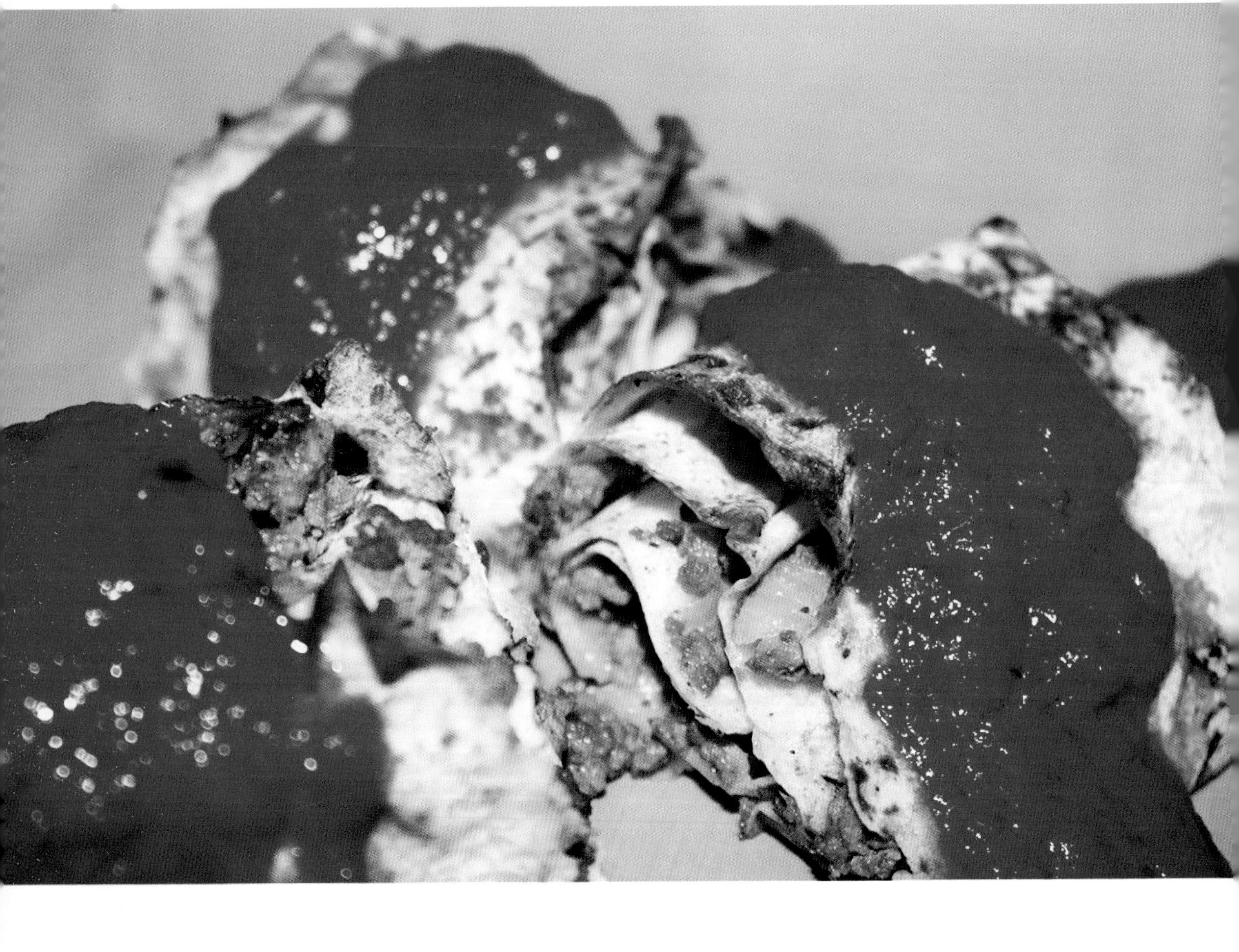

INGREDIENTS

2 lb ground beef

1 large onion (finely chopped)

Salt and pepper to taste

½ c milk

½ c water

½ c oil

12 pieces lavash

4 tbsp butter

2 tbsp tomato paste

¼ c water

PREPARATION

Preheat oven to 350°F. Brown ground beef with onion. Season to taste with salt and pepper. Mix milk, water and oil and brush approximately 1 tbsp of milk,water,and oil mixture on a piece of lavash. Then spread one twelfth of the ground beef filling (make sure beef is distributed evenly), roll tightly, and cut into 1" slices. Place lavash rolls seam-side down in a 9" x 13" baking dish. Continue with all the other lavash breads and bake them for 20 minutes.

Melt butter and add tomato paste. Cook over medium heat for 2-3 minutes and then add water. Pour over all lavash in the pan before serving. Serve it on top of beyti kebab. You can also broil tomatoes or green peppers to serve with beyti kebab.

STUFFED ZUCCHINIS (ETLI KABAK DOLMASI)****

INGREDIENTS

Stuffing:

½ lb ground beef

½ c rice (rinsed and drained)

1 tomato (grated)

1 onion (chopped)

1 tsp dried mint

Salt and pepper to taste

½ tsp fresh dill

1 tbsp tomato paste

1 tbsp red pepper paste

6 zucchinis

Hot water

On Top:

3 tbsp butter

1 tomato (diced)

PREPARATION

Mix stuffing ingredients thoroughly. Wash the zucchinis and cut from the middle into two pieces, scrape out the inside with a small spoon. Stuff the zucchinis and leave some room (about ¼ inch) at the top. Lay the stuffed zucchinis in a pot. Dot each one with ¼ tsp of butter and top with diced tomatoes. From the side of the pan, gently add an inch of water at. Bring it to a boil, lower the heat, cover and cook for about 30 minutes.

IZMIR KOFTE***

INGREDIENTS

1 lb ground beef

1 small onion (grated)

½ c bread crumbs

1 egg

Salt and pepper to taste

4-5 potatoes

2 tbsp olive oil

2 tbsp butter

¼ c tomato paste

2 c water

Salt to taste

PREPARATION

Preheat oven to 350°F. Mix ground beef with grated onion, bread crumbs, egg, salt and pepper. Form into logs about ½" in diameter and 3" in length. Line a 9"x13" baking dish with parchment paper and bake for 20 minutes. Transfer meatballs to a plate. Increase oven temperature to 400°F. Peel and slice the potatoes into ½ inch thick. and mix with 2 tbsp olive oil. Remove parchment paper from the baking dish used for the meatballs, put potatoes in it, and bake for 25 minutes. In a large pan, melt the butter and mix with tomato paste and cook for 5 minutes over medium heat. Add water and salt and bring to a boil. Place the potatoes with the kofte into the tomato sauce and cook for 5 more minutes.

TURKISH RAVIOLI (MANTI)*****

PREPARATION

INGREDIENTS

Sumac and dried mint (optional)

Filling:
1 lb low-fat ground beef

Salt and pepper to taste

½ onion (grated)

1 tsp tomato paste

Dough:
2 eggs

3 c flour (If needed you may add more flour to get a hard dough)

⅔ c water

Salt to taste

5 c water

Salt to taste

Sauce:
1 or 2 cloves of garlic to taste (minced)

16 oz yogurt

4 tbsp butter

1 tbsp tomato paste

¼ c water

To make the filling, mix ground beef well with salt and pepper. Add onion, tomato paste and mix with your hands a little more. Wash your hands and make the dough: combine flour and salt in a mixing bowl. Add egg and water and knead well until you get a smooth, hard dough. Roll the dough out into a ⅛″ thick circle. Cut dough into 1″ squares. Place a pea-sized amount of filling in the middle of each. Seal the ravioli ("manti") by gathering the edges of the dough and pinching them together at the top to form a bundle. Transfer the finished ravioli to a floured plate, and sprinkle more flour over the ravioli to prevent them from sticking to each other. (If you want to save the ravioli for later you can bake in a preheated 350°F oven for about 10-15 minutes until lightly browned, cool, and freeze them in zip-top bags.)

Bring 5 cups of salted water to a boil over medium-high heat. Shake excess flour from the raviolis and add them to gently boiling water. Cook for about 15 minutes stirring occasionally. You know they are done when they float.

Mix garlic with yogurt and set aside. Melt butter in a small skillet and add tomato paste, cook for 2-3 minutes, and then add water. Remove from the heat and keep warm. Transfer cooked raviolis to a serving plate using a slotted spoon. Some people like to drain their raviolis completely, and some people like to serve their ravioli with a bit of cooking water; adjust according to your taste. Pour some yogurt sauce over the ravioli and drizzle with the hot tomato sauce. You may also garnish with sumac and dried mint.

ALI NAZIK KEBAB (ALI NAZIK KEBABI)***

INGREDIENTS

3 eggplants (globe)

2 tbsp oil

1 tbsp butter

1 onion (chopped)

1 tsp tomato paste (or red pepper paste)

1 lb ground beef

¼ c water

Salt and pepper to taste

2 cloves garlic (minced)

Salt

1½ c plain yogurt

To garnish:

Parsley

Roasted tomatoes

Roasted Anaheim peppers

The Story of Ali Nazik Kebab

According to legend, in the 16th century, when Sultan Yavuz Selim came to Antep, there were ceremonies and celebrations to welcome him. Along with numerous dedications to the sultan, lots of food was made for him. The Ali Nazik dish was in between hundreds of other dishes. The sultan, mesmerized by the dish, said "Whose gentle hands ("Eli Nazik") made this dish?" The name was passed down as Ali Nazik and remains that to this day.

Preheat oven to 375°F. Pierce eggplants in several places and bake for 40 minutes. Allow to cool, peel and mash with a fork. Set aside.

Heat oil and butter in a pan. Add chopped onion and cook until light brown. Add tomato paste and stir briefly. Add ground beef and then water. Add salt and pepper while the ground beef is cooking.

In a deep thoroughly bowl mix minced garlic, salt and yogurt. Add eggplant and mix in well. To serve pour some yogurt-eggplant mixture onto a plate and put ground beef on top. Serve with parsley, roasted tomatoes and roasted peppers on the side.

CLAY POT LAMB AND VEGGIES (COMLEK KEBABI)***

INGREDIENTS

Clay pot (or Dutch Oven)

5-6 eggplants (peeled and cubed) (Japanese)

2 medium onions (chopped)

2 lb lamb (cut in ⅔ inch cubes)

2 tbsp olive oil

1-2 bell peppers (chopped)

2 potatoes (cubed)

1 zucchini (cubed)

2 cloves garlic (chopped)

2 tomatoes (grated)

1 bunch parsley

2 tbsp butter

Salt and pepper to taste

1½ c hot water

PREPARATION

Preheat oven to 325°F. Soak the eggplant in salty water. Add the onions to the clay pot with cubed lamb. Add olive oil. Add chopped bell peppers, eggplant, potato, zucchini, garlic and tomato and a bunch of parsley. On top add butter, salt, pepper and finally the hot water. Cover the clay pot with parchment paper and put the lid on. Bake for 2 hours. Check after 90 minutes; if it looks, dry add more hot water. Remove the parsley before serving.

SULTAN'S DELIGHT (HUNKAR BEGENDI)***

PREPARATION

INGREDIENTS

1 lb beef (thinly sliced)

1 medium onion (chopped)

2 tomatoes (peeled and diced into small cubes)

Salt and pepper to taste

Béchamel Sauce with Eggplants:

2 globe eggplants, approx. 8 oz each

4 tbsp butter

3 tbsp flour

2 c milk

Salt to taste

1 c mozzarella (shredded)

To garnish:

Parsley leaves (optional)

Place the beef in a lightly oiled pan and cook over medium heat until the juices have evaporated. Add the onion and cook until lightly browned. Stir in diced tomatoes, salt and pepper. Reduce heat to low and cook until the beef is tender. Add a bit of water if necessary. Pierce the eggplants with a fork in several places and broil for 30-40 minutes (turning occasionally) in oven until they are softened. Let them cool, peel, and mash them with a fork. Melt the butter in a saucepan. Add flour and lightly brown it, stirring constantly for 1 minute. Whisk in the milk, stirring constantly until the sauce reaches a creamy consistency. Season to taste with salt. Add mashed eggplant to the sauce, blend and cook for 2-3 minutes. Stir in the cheese. Mix well and turn the heat off. Pour the eggplant sauce onto a serving plate and top with the meat. You may garnish with parsley leaves.

The Story of Sultan's Delight

'Hunkar begendi' means the dish the "Sultan liked", and when it comes to the specific sultan that initiated the dish, we acknowledge two different stories. The first is as follows. The Ottoman palace kitchen included chefs with years of experience who tried to satisfy the sultan, working day and night to achieve wonders, and finally made a brilliant new dish. It was made during the time period 1612-1640 and presented to Sultan Murat Han IV; he was fascinated by it. The word came to the kitchen about the sultan liking the dish, so the chef named it hunkar begendi. The second story is more recent. In the late 1800s, Sultan Abdulaziz invited special guests to his palace, the French king Napoleon III and Queen Eugenie, who were visiting Istanbul at the time. The sultan requested only the best foods to be made. Finally, the chefs succeed in making a dish that satisfied the sultan, and they named it "hunkar begendi."

MEATBALLS WITH RICE (KADINBUDU KOFTE)***

INGREDIENTS

1 small onion (chopped)

2 tbsp vegetable oil

1 lb ground beef (divided in half)

¼ c white rice

¾ c water

1 egg

Salt, pepper and cumin (to taste)

For coating the meatballs:

2 eggs

½ c flour

Oil (to fry)

PREPARATION

Sauté the onion in vegetable oil. Add half of the ground beef and cook it until the juices evaporate. Set aside to cool. Meanwhile cook the rice with the water and drain it. Combine the cooked rice, cooked beef with onion, egg, salt, pepper, cumin, and the remaining uncooked beef. Knead it and chill for half an hour. Form into egg sized oblong meatballs. Beat two eggs in a small bowl. Place the flour on a plate, and heat the oil in a pan. Roll the meatballs first in flour and then in beaten egg. Fry over high heat until golden brown. Drain on paper towel and serve hot with vegetables.

DRY BEANS WITH SAUSAGE (SUCUKLU KURU FASULYE)***

INGREDIENTS

2 c dry Great Northern beans

4 c water (to soak beans)

Water to cover (for boiling)

1 medium onion (chopped)

1 tbsp tomato paste

1 tbsp pepper paste

5 tbsp vegetable oil

1 c hot water (for cooking)

½ lb Turkish sausage (soujuk)

1 tsp salt

PREPARATION

Soak dry beans overnight in 4 cups water. The next day, drain them, rinse, and put in a pot. Add water to cover the beans by two inches. Add salt and let it boil. When it boils, lower the heat, cover, and cook for 1 ½ hours or until the beans are softened. Drain and set aside. In a different pan, briefly saute onion, tomato paste, and pepper paste in vegetable oil. Add beans, hot water and cook for 10 minutes. Meanwhile cut the sausages in half, slice thinly and saute in another pan. Stir in sausages and salt to the beans. Serve with pilaf.

LAMB KEBAB (KUZU KEBAP)**

INGREDIENTS

1 lb lamb meat (1 inch cubed)

2 tbsp olive oil

1½ tsp tomato paste

1 tbsp red pepper paste

Salt (to taste)

1 tsp crushed red pepper flakes

¼ c water

1 lb pearl onion

1 tbsp butter

PREPARATION

Cook lamb cubes in a dry pan over low heat until juices evaporate. Add olive oil, tomato paste, pepper paste, salt, crushed red pepper flakes and sauté for 2-3 min. Add water and bring to a boil. Reduce heat to simmer and cover. Stir occasionally; cook until lamb is tender. Sauté pearl onions in butter until softened and add to cooked lamb. Cook for 2-3 more minutes.

CHICKEN SHISH KEBAB (TAVUK SIS)**

PREPARATION

Put all of the ingredients except the chicken in a bowl and mix them well. Add the chicken and toss together. Marinate in the fridge for a minimum of 1 hour and as much as overnight. Preheat oven to 400°F. Place 6 chicken cubes on each skewer. Optionally you may place tomato, eggplant, green pepper or onion slices in between chicken cubes. Bake at 400°F for about 25 minutes, turning occasionally.

INGREDIENTS

½ tbsp red pepper paste

½ tbsp tomato paste

½ c water

2-3 tbsp olive oil

Salt and pepper to taste

½ tsp cumin powder

½ tsp dried mint

1 tsp red pepper flakes

3-4 boneless, skinless chicken thighs (cut in 1 inch cubes)

12 Skewers, soaked in water for 1 hour if wooden

TANTUNI (TANTUNI KEBAP)**

INGREDIENTS

2 lb beef (diced)

¼ c oil

Salt and pepper to taste

Uncooked tortilla

Onion-tomato salad (see "Side Dishes" chapter)

Pickles (optional)

PREPARATION

Brown the beef in oil at high heat and then reduce the heat to low. Cover and cook 30 minutes until the meat is very soft and has absorbed its juice. Season to taste with salt and pepper. Meanwhile, heat a large non-stick frying pan and lightly brown the uncooked tortillas on each side. Place 2 tablespoons of beef and onion-tomato salad into the tortillas and roll it up. Serve with pickles and ayran.

LAMB STEW WITH PRUNES (KURU ERIK YAHNISI)**

INGREDIENTS

1 c prunes

2 lb lamb meat (diced)

2 c water

¼ c olive oil or 2 tbsp butter

1½ c pearl onion (peeled)

1 tsp cinnamon

1 tsp sugar

1 tsp salt

PREPARATION

Soak prunes in water to cover for 2 hours. Cook meat in a pan with 2 cups of water and let it boil. Cover and reduce the heat to low, and continue cooking about 30 minutes more until the lamb is tender. Add olive oil or butter to a deep pot. Add meat, peeled shallots and cook over medium heat for 10 minutes. Add drained prunes, cinnamon, sugar, salt and cover. Let it cook for 5 more minutes.

STUFFED COLLARD GREENS (KIYMALI KARA LAHANA SARMASI)*****

INGREDIENTS

2 bunches collard greens

4 qt water

Filling:

1 onion (chopped)

1 c rice (rinsed and drained)

½ lb ground beef

1 tbsp tomato paste

1 c fresh parsley (finely chopped)

½ tsp black pepper

½ tsp crushed red pepper

½ c corn oil

1 tbsp tomato paste

Salt (to taste)

Hot water

PREPARATION

Wash the collards well in cold water. Remove the center stem by slicing along either side of it with a knife. In a 5 qt pot, boil the water and dip the leaves in it for about 1 minute. Then, drain and cool. Keep 2-3 large leaves whole but cut the remaining large leaves into three triangular pieces and cut the smaller ones into two. To prepare the filling, combine all the filling ingredients in a bowl. Take one leaf and place 1 tsp of filling on a larger side. Then, fold the other sides in and roll up. Repeat for all leaves. Sauté the corn oil and tomato paste in a saucepan. Put the reserved whole collard greens in the bottom of a pot and place all the rolls side by side. Pour the tomato paste-oil mixture on the rolled leaves. Put a porcelain plate upside down on top of the rolls to prevent unrolling. Add hot water just to cover the rolls. Bring to a boil over medium heat. Then, decrease the heat to a simmer and cover. Cook for about 40 minutes or until the rolls are tender.

MEATBALL STEW (KOFTE YAHNISI)***

INGREDIENTS

1 big onion (divided in half)

2 lb ground beef

½ c rice (rinsed)

Salt and pepper to taste

½ tsp cumin

1 egg

4 cloves garlic

¼ c corn oil

1 tbsp tomato paste

½ tbsp pepper paste

4-5 bay leaves

4 c water

PREPARATION

Chop one half of the onion. Mix it with ground beef, rice, salt, pepper, cumin, egg and knead for 3-5 minutes. Take walnut sized pieces of the mixture and shape them into balls. Chop the remaining onion and garlic and sauté in corn oil until golden brown. Then add tomato and pepper paste and cook for 1-2 minutes. Lastly, stir in bay leaves, and add the water and bring to a boil. When it boils, add the meatballs, return to a boil, then lower heat to simmer. Cover and cook until the grains of rice expand as they cook.

MEATLOAF (RULO KOFTE)****

INGREDIENTS

1 lb ground beef (93% lean)

½ c bread crumbs

2 eggs

1 tsp black pepper

1 tsp dried oregano

Crushed red pepper flakes to taste

Salt to taste

½ c chopped parsley

1-15 oz can mixed vegetables, drained

Salt to taste

3 hard-boiled eggs

1 egg white (whisked)

4 tbsp butter

PREPARATION

Preheat oven to 400°F. Mix ground beef, bread crumbs, eggs, spices and parsley. Mix with your hands for 3-5 minutes. Place in a greased 9″x13″ baking pan and flatten to 1 inch. Place the mixed vegetables onto the meat and sprinkle with salt. Next place whole boiled eggs lengthwise in a row down the middle. Carefully draw up the two 13″ sides of the meat to join in the middle and enclose the vegetables and eggs. Gently turn so the seam side is down. Brush the surface with one whisked egg white. Dot the top with 4 tablespoons of butter. Bake for 40 minutes. Check on the meatloaf during baking, occasionally basting it with the juices it releases.

ZUCCHINI GRATIN (KABAK GRATEN)**

INGREDIENTS

4 zucchinis

1 boneless, skinless chicken breast (cut into ½" cubes)

1 tbsp olive oil

1 onion (chopped)

1 garlic clove (chopped)

Salt and pepper to taste

Crushed red pepper flakes

½ tsp curry powder

½ bunch Dill (finely chopped)

⅔ c grated mozzarella cheese

Olive oil

Béchamel Sauce with Nutmeg:

2 tbsp butter

2 tbsp flour

1 c milk

Salt and pepper (to taste)

¼ tsp nutmeg

PREPARATION

Preheat oven to 350°F. Wash zucchinis and cut vertically into two pieces, scrape out the inside with a small spoon. Place zucchinis in a saucepan and cover with water. Boil them 5-7 minutes, drain, cool under running water, and drain on paper towels. For the filling, sauté the chicken in olive oil. Add onion, garlic, salt, pepper, crushed red pepper flakes, curry powder and saute together. Turn off the heat and add dill. Stuff zucchinis with this mixture. For béchamel sauce, melt butter in a pan; add flour and sauté until lightly brown. Slowly stir in milk. As sauce becomes thicker add salt, pepper and nutmeg. With a spoon, spread the sauce on top of the stuffed zucchinis. Sprinkle grated mozzarella cheese on top. Bake about 30 minutes.

CHICKEN KAPAMA (TAVUK KAPAMA)*****

INGREDIENTS

Dough:

1½ c milk (warm)

1 tbsp instant yeast

1 egg •1 tsp salt •⅓ c oil

½ tsp dried mint

1 c parsley (finely chopped)

1 tsp sugar •3½ c flour

Oil for frying

Stuffing ingredients:

2 chicken breasts (diced)

1 onion (chopped) •2 tbsp oil

1 tsp curry powder

½ tsp chili powder

Salt and pepper to taste

1 garlic clove (chopped)

Yogurt Sauce:

2¼ c yogurt •Salt

1 garlic clove (grated)

Tomato Sauce:

2 tbsp butter

1 tbsp tomato paste

½ tsp mint

PREPARATION

Dissolve yeast in warm milk. Add egg, salt, oil, mint, parsley, sugar and flour and mix to make a non-sticky dough. Separate the dough into 10 pieces and form balls. Cover with a damp cloth and let them sit while you prepare the stuffing. Sauté onion with oil, add chicken, spices, and garlic and sauté together until browned. Set aside to cool. Roll out each of two pieces of dough into a 10″ circle. Put 3 tbsp chicken stuffing onto one dough piece, spread evenly to within 1″ of the edge, and put the other dough on top. Seal the edges by crimping with a fork. Repeat with remaining 8 pieces of dough. Heat about 1 tbsp of oil in a large frying pan. Fry each kapama on both sides until browned. Mix yogurt, garlic and salt. In a small pan, melt 2 tbsp butter. Stir in tomato paste and mint. To serve, put one chicken kapama on a plate; place some yogurt sauce on the center and top with some tomato sauce. Slice into wedges and serve.

PEAS WITH CHICKEN (TAVUKLU BEZELYE)***

INGREDIENTS

1 medium onion (chopped)

¼ c corn oil

1 lb chicken breast

1 tbsp tomato paste

3 tomatoes (cut into ½" dice)

1 carrot (cut into ½" dice)

1 medium potato (cut into ½" dice)

1 lb peas (frozen)

2 c water

Salt and pepper to taste

Red pepper flakes and black pepper (optional)

2 tbsp fresh dill (chopped)

PREPARATION

Saute onions in oil for 3 minutes. Add chicken breast and saute 5-7 more minutes. Add tomato paste and tomatoes and saute 5 more minutes. Add carrots, potatoes and peas, and saute for 3 more minutes. Then add water and spices, bring to a boil, reduce heat to simmer, cover, and cook for 30 to 40 more minutes. Add dill and cook for 5 more minutes before serving.

OKRA AND LAMB STEW (ETLI BAMYA)**

INGREDIENTS

1 lb baby okra (frozen)

6 c water

Juice of ½ lemon

2 tbsp oil

½ lb lamb (diced)

1 large onion (chopped)

2 tomatoes, peeled and chopped

1 tbsp tomato paste

1 c water

Salt to taste

PREPARATION

Rinse okra and soak in the water with lemon juice for about 30 minutes. Drain, rinse, and set aside. Add oil to a saucepan and cook lamb at medium heat until the juice evaporates. Stir in onion, and cook for 10 more minutes. Add tomato, tomato paste, and 1 cup water. Stir to mix and reduce heat to low. Cook the mixture for about 20 minutes. Add okra and cook until okra and meat are at desired tenderness.

ROLLED PHYLOS WITH CHICKEN (ZIRON)**

INGREDIENTS

3 pieces of Turkish phyllo dough

1 lb boneless, skinless chicken thigh

8 c water

1½ tsp salt

2 c yogurt

2 garlic cloves (minced)

2 tbsp butter

1 tsp red pepper flakes

PREPARATION

Preheat oven to 400°F. Tightly roll one sheet of phyllo dough. Cut into 1" slices and place the rolls on a lightly oiled baking pan with cut side facing up. Repeat for remaining pieces of phyllo dough. Bake them about 30 minutes, until golden brown. In the meantime, boil chicken in the water with salt for 15 minutes. Drain the boiled chicken, reserving the broth. Cool, and then shred the chicken. Pour the reserved chicken broth onto baked phyllos and let it sit for 3 minutes. Mix yogurt with garlic and pour on top of the phyllos. Next spread the shredded chicken on top. Melt butter in a pan and boil for minute. Stir in the red pepper flakes and pour on top of the chicken and serve immediately.

SAUTEED MUSHROOMS (MANTAR SOTE)**

INGREDIENTS

4 c crimini mushrooms

1 lb sweet mini peppers (sliced and seeded)

2 tbsp olive oil

4 medium tomatoes (chopped or shredded)

Salt and pepper to taste

½ tsp dried oregano

PREPARATION

Wash mushrooms, trim the ends, remove the stems from the caps, and slice the caps only. Discard the stems. . Heat olive oil in a pot. Add sliced mushroom. Let them saute until they absorb their liquid. Add sliced sweet mini peppers. Saute for about 2 minutes. Add tomatoes, salt, pepper and oregano. Saute until liquid is absorbed. You can serve this as a side dish along with meat, chicken or fish.

PAN-FRIED ANCHOVIES (HAMSI TAVA)**

INGREDIENTS

1 c corn flour

Salt (to taste)

2 lb uncooked anchovies (cleaned and rinsed)

2 tsp corn oil

1 tsp butter

PREPARATION

Mix corn flour and salt in a large bowl. Coat the fish with the mixture and shake off excess. Heat oil and butter in a frying pan with a diameter about twice the length of an anchovy. Brown anchovies, aligning them so they touch and the heads face the center. Once one side is browned, carefully flip the group of anchovies intact and fry the other side. Add more oil to the pan if needed.

Anchovies and the Dance of 'Horon'

The Black Sea region of Turkey is very rich in anchovies, and the people of this region make almost any kind of dish using anchovies: anchovy rice pilaf, steamed anchovies, anchovy bread, and anchovy cake, to name a few of them. The people of this region are known for being hyperactive; it seems they cannot sit still. It is said that this hyperactivity is similar to that of the anchovies jumping in the net after being caught. This region has a very unique and extremely difficult dance called the 'horon' which involves jumping and rapid upper body movements, again resembling anchovies jumping in the net.. The style is similar to Greek and Persian dancing, and it's thought that the Irish jig (and its modern form, the River Dance) may be related. Eating lots of fish and dancing the horon, these people are very healthy and thin.

BAKED TROUT (FIRINDA ALABALIK) (2 SERVING)*

INGREDIENTS

1 Trout (about 1 lb)

Seasoning:

Salt and pepper to taste, crushed red pepper, oregano

Olive oil

Juice of ½ lemon

2 finely chopped tomatoes

½ green bell pepper (diced)

½ c parsley leaves

PREPARATION

Preheat oven to 350°F. Clean the fish, leaving the head and skin on. Wash the trout and marinate with seasonings. Place in a baking dish. Lay the tomatoes, bell pepper, and parsley leaves on the fish. Bake approximately 30 minutes, until tender. You may also bake the trout in a clay pot as pictured.

BAKED MACKEREL (KIREMITTE PALAMUT)*

INGREDIENTS

2 Mackerel, skin on, total about 1 lb

Seasoning:

Salt and pepper to taste

½ tsp crushed red pepper flakes

½ tsp oregano

1 tbsp olive oil

Juice of ½ lemon

2 finely chopped tomatoes

½ green bell pepper (thinly sliced)

½ c parsley (chopped)

PREPARATION

Preheat oven to 350°F. Clean the fish leaving the skin on. Cut mackerel into 1 inch slices, marinate with seasoning for 10 minutes. Place fish in a baking dish. Sprinkle with chopped tomatoes, green bell pepper and parsley leaves. Bake until tender, approximately 30 minutes. You may also bake the fish in a clay pot as pictured.

TURKIC DISHES

Rich variety of dishes from
the Balkans, Caucasus
and Central Asia

BLACK EYED PEA AND NOODLE SOUP (UNASH)***** (TURKMENISTAN)

INGREDIENTS

¾ c canned black eyed peas (drained and rinsed)

4 c water

1½ tbsp tomato paste (or 2 peeled diced tomatoes)

Salt and pepper to taste

Homemade noodles (see recipe below)

Yogurt (optional)

Crushed red pepper flakes (optional)

Homemade noodles:

½ c water

1 tsp salt

2 c flour

PREPARATION

Noodle preparation:

Make non-sticky dough of medium softness, adding flour slowly. Roll out the dough very thin (approximately ¼ inches), flouring as needed to prevent sticking. Roll up the dough and cut ⅛"slices to create noodles. Cut noodles to desired length.

Boil black eyed peas in 4 cups water until tender, about 20 minutes. Next add tomato paste, salt and pepper, boiling for 5-10 more minutes. Add water if needed. Then add homemade noodles, cooking 2-3 minutes until done. Garnish each serving with 1-2 tbsp yogurt and crushed red pepper flakes before serving.

MIMOSA SALAD (MIMOZA SALATASI)*** (MIDDLE ASIA)

INGREDIENTS

4 potatoes

4 carrots

5 eggs

1 onion (chopped)

1-2 tbsp oil

2-3.5 oz cans chunk tuna

22 oz squeeze bottle mayonnaise

Salt to taste

Parsley or dill (optional)

PREPARATION

Boil potatoes, carrots and eggs until cooked. Cool and peel. Sauté onion with oil and cool. Grate potatoes and carrots. Grate egg whites and yolks separately. Start putting grated ingredients in a serving dish in layers in order listed below or as you wish with mayonnaise squeezed in strips 1" apart top to bottom for one layer and then side to side for the next layer: potatoes, tuna, onion, carrots, egg white and then finally egg yolk. You may garnish with parsley or dill.

TURKMEN SOUP (TURKMEN CORBASI)** (TURKMENISTAN)

INGREDIENTS

½ lb beef (cut into ½" chunks)

1 c water

2-3 tbsp oil

½ medium onion (chopped)

1 tbsp tomato paste or 2 fresh tomatoes

2 tbsp green bell pepper (chopped)

5 c water

Salt and pepper to taste

2 medium potatoes (cut in ½" cubes)

1 carrot (chopped)

PREPARATION

Put beef chunks in a pot over medium heat and add 1 cup of water. Bring to a boil, and let the liquid boil away. Then add oil and sauté, still over medium heat, until meat is tender. Add chopped onion, tomato paste, bell pepper and sauté together. Add 5 cups of water, salt and pepper and bring to a boil. Then, add potatoes and carrot to the soup, bring to a boil, and simmer until they are tender, adding water as needed.

SALAD WITH YOGURT AND SOUR CREAM (KAJMAK SALAD)** (BOSNIA)

INGREDIENTS

4 tomatoes

6 cucumbers

Fresh dill

1 red onion

2 garlic cloves

1 c sour cream

1 c yogurt

Salt and pepper to taste

PREPARATION

Wash tomatoes and cucumbers and rinse dill. Then peel onion, garlic, and cucumbers. Slice cucumbers, tomatoes and onion; chop garlic and dill. Mix sour cream and yogurt in a bowl. Then add chopped dill and garlic, then salt and pepper, mix together. Stir in tomatoes, cucumbers and onion until combined.

CIRCASSIAN CHICKEN (CERKEZ TAVUGU)***

INGREDIENTS

Half a chicken breast (boneless and skinless)

1 c walnuts (finely chopped)

1 c plain yogurt

½ c mayonnaise

1 clove garlic (minced)

½ c bread crumbs

1 bunch dill (finely chopped)

¼ c olive oil

1 tbsp lemon juice

1 tsp salt

PREPARATION

Boil chicken breast until tender. Drain, cool, and shred. Mix thoroughly with all other ingredients. Circassian chicken can be served at room temperature as a salad or a sandwich spread.

TURKMEN BREAD (TURKMEN EKMEGI)***

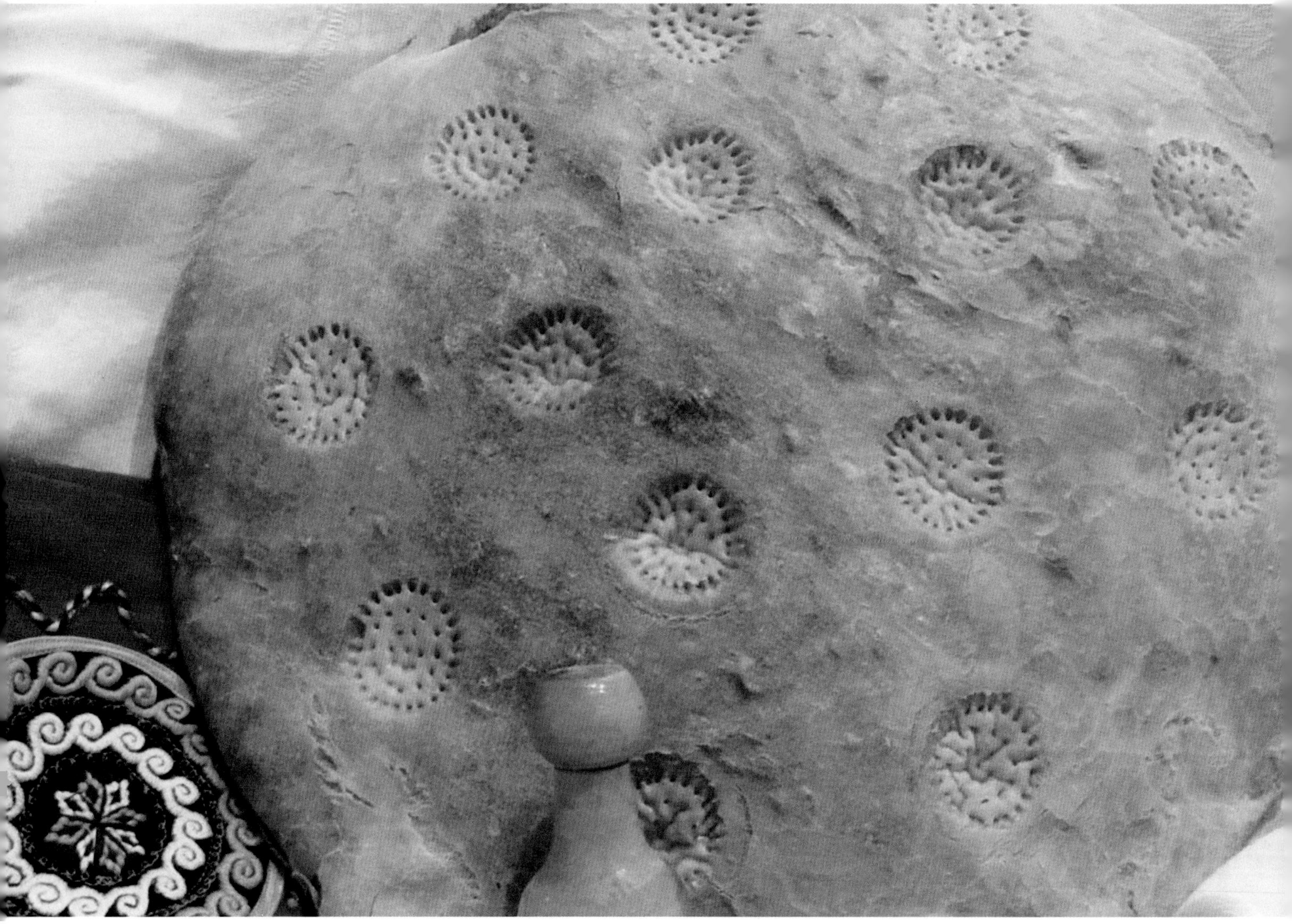

INGREDIENTS

2 c water (warm)

1 c milk (warm)

1 tbsp salt

1 tbsp instant yeast

7 c flour

Non-stick cooking spray

¼ c water

PREPARATION

Combine water, milk, and salt in a deep bowl. Dissolve yeast in it. Slowly mix in flour to make a non-sticky soft dough. Adjust the amount of water or flour as needed. Cover the dough with a clean cloth and let it sit for 30 minutes. Grease a 13″x18″ baking pan. Roll out the dough into a 1″-1½″ thick circle. Place on the baking pan, cover, and let it rise for an hour. In the meantime, preheat oven to 400°F. To obtain the Turkmen bread design on top, gently press on the dough with the traditional Turkmen Bread shaper or with a fork. Then brush top of the bread with ¼ cup water to make the bread softer. Bake until golden brown, approximately 30 minutes.

ALBANIAN PASTRY (ARNAVUT BOREGI)***

INGREDIENTS

Dough:

3½ c flour

1½ c water

1 tsp salt

1 tbsp vinegar

Filling:

5 leeks

1 medium onion

¼ c corn oil

½ tbsp salt

1 tsp black pepper

1 tsp red pepper flakes

1½ c butter (melted)

PREPARATION

Place the flour in a mixing bowl, making a well. Add water, salt, and vinegar to the well and knead until you have a non-sticky dough, adding flour as needed. Knead well and divide into 22 pieces. Cover with a damp cloth and let the dough rest. To prepare the filling, clean the leeks thoroughly. Slice the leeks and onion very thinly. Sauté onion in oil until translucent. Then stir in the chopped leeks and sauté until they release and absorb their liquid. Cool. Finally, mix in salt, black pepper and red pepper flakes.

Preheat oven to 350°F. Take one dough piece, sift some flour on it and roll out to 6″ in diameter. Repeat this process with the remaining 21 pieces. Brush the first piece evenly with about 1 tbsp of melted butter. Place the second piece of dough on top and brush it with butter as well. Repeat the process until you have a stack 11 layers high. Repeat the procedure with the other 11 pieces to make a second stack. Carefully roll out one stack to a little bigger than the pan and place on a greased 13″x18″ baking pan. Spread the filling mixture on top. Roll out the second stack a little smaller than pan and place on top of the filling. Fold the edges of the bottom crust towards the center, pressing to seal with the upper crust. Cut a few slits in the top crust to allow steam to escape during baking. Bake until golden brown. After taking out of the oven, carefully place a clean, damp cloth on top and let it rest for 3-4 minutes. Slice and serve hot.

FRIED PASTRY (CIG BOREK) (KIRGIZISTAN)****

INGREDIENTS

Dough:

3 c flour

1 tsp salt

2 c warm water

Filling:

½ lb ground beef

1 small onion (chopped thinly)

½ tsp ground black pepper

½ tsp salt

2 tbsp cold water

PREPARATION

Vegetable oil for frying

Knead the dough ingredients together until firm, adding water or flour as needed. Cover with a damp cloth and let the dough sit for about 30 minutes. Make golf ball sized balls of dough. Sift some flour on the counter and roll each ball to 6" in diameter. Mix filling ingredients. Put one tablespoon of the raw filling on one half of each dough and spread thinly. Fold the dough circle in half. Press on the edges with your fingers or tines of a fork to seal. Heat oil and deep fry until light golden brown on each side.

FRIED PIROJKI WITH POTATOES (PATATESLI HAMUR KIZARTMASI - MIDDLE ASIA)****

INGREDIENTS

Dough:

2¼ c water (or milk)

1 tbsp yeast

1 egg (optional)

1 tbsp sugar

7 - 7½ c flour

1½ tsp salt

Filling:

1 lb potatoes

1 onion (chopped)

6 tbsp oil

½ tbsp salt

½ tsp black pepper

PREPARATION

Vegetable oil for frying

Mix all dough ingredients together and make soft dough, using 7 cups of flour first then adding another ½ cup if needed (You can use a bread machine). Cover the dough with a damp cloth and let it stand for 30 minutes to 1 hour.. Peel and dice potatoes, putting them on to boil. Meanwhile, sauté chopped onion in oil. Once potatoes are tender, drain and mash with the sautéd onion and oil, mixing in salt and pepper. Take golf ball sized pieces of dough, flatten a little (to about 3" in diameter) with your hand and put 1 tbsp filling in the middle. Then fold in half, pinching the edges to seal. Heat oil and fry pirojki until golden brown. Drain on paper towel before serving.

TURKMEN SHEPHERD PIE (ISHLEKLI)*** (TURKMENISTAN)

INGREDIENTS

Dough:

3½ c flour

1 c lukewarm water

1 tsp salt

½ tsp baking soda

For the filling:

1 lb ground beef

1 tomato, diced

½ bell pepper, diced

1 onion, finely chopped

1 potato, diced

1 tsp salt

1 pinch black pepper

1 pinch red chili pepper

½ c water

PREPARATION

Non-stick spray or parchment paper

Mix the dough ingredients, kneading to form a soft, smooth dough. Next, mix the filling ingredients well with a spoon. Preheat the oven 450°F. Grease a 16″ pizza pan. Separate the dough into two balls, one a little larger than the other. Roll them out into ¼″ thick circles. Put the larger piece on the pizza pan and spread the filling evenly over the dough, up to1½″ from the edge. Place the smaller dough on top. Fold the larger bottom dough on top of the smaller dough and pinch or crimp with a fork to seal. Cut a few steam holes in the top dough. Bake 25 minutes or until golden brown. Brush with butter, cover with foil, and leave to cool. In Turkmenistan, Ishlekli is traditionally served with green tea.

SHEET PASTRY WITH LEEKS (PIRASALI CARSAF BOREGI)***** (BOSNIA)

INGREDIENTS

3 c bread flour (for easier stretching)

1 c water (warm)

Salt to taste

Vegetable oil to brush on dough while it rests

Filling:

1 medium onion (chopped)

2 tbsp vegetable oil

3 bunches of leeks (finely chopped)

2 tbsp tomato paste

Salt and pepper to taste

3 tbsp yogurt

2 egg yolks

PREPARATION

Preheat oven to 350°F. Put the flour, warm water and salt in a bowl and knead to form smooth and firm dough, adding flour or water as needed. Take tennis ball sized pieces of dough and roll each to 8″ diameter. Place on a greased baking pan and brush with a generous amount of oil so that the dough does not dry out. Let them sit for 30 minutes. Meanwhile, prepare the filling. Clean leeks well. Sauté chopped onion with oil and add the finely chopped leeks. Add tomato paste, salt and pepper and sauté for another minute. Put one of the flattened doughs on a clean tablecloth and flatten it by stretching as thin as you can with your hands, maintaining a generally round shape. Then place the filling over the dough. Roll it up. Place it on greased baking pan and form into a spiral. Put the pastry on the baking pan and start baking. Whisk together yogurt and egg yolks. After 15 minutes in the oven, remove the pastry and brush with this mixture, then bake for an additional 45 minutes.

BOSNIAN PASTRY WITH SPINACH*****

INGREDIENTS

Filling:

16 oz cottage cheese

1 c feta cheese (crumbled)

4 eggs

1 c sour cream

Salt to taste

Green onion (diced)

2 lb fresh spinach (washed and cut)

1 tbsp cornmeal (to be sprinkled on the pan)

½ c butter

Dough:

2 lb bread flour 1 tbsp salt

½ c vegetable oil

Warm water (as needed)

PREPARATION

Preheat the oven 450°F then decrease to 425°F. Mix together all filling ingredients except butter. In another mixing bowl put flour, salt, oil, and water. Knead and add water as needed to form a soft dough. Divide dough into 3 pieces (or more if you have a small table), and let sit for 15 min. Then on a clean cotton table cloth, start rolling out the first dough ball. Brush vegetable oil on the dough, and let it sit for a few minutes. Next, stretch dough as big as a table (or even bigger, so it drapes over like a table cloth), until you can see through the dough. (This is better performed with two people.) Spread the filling close to the edges of the table. Cut the dough in the middle. Roll up the dough from the edge towards the center. Then cut each roll into 4-5 pieces and swirl the dough to obtain an elongated G shape. Lightly grease the baking pan and sprinkle with cornmeal. Place the dough pieces on the pan and brush with butter. Bake for 20 minutes until golden brown.

STEAMED RAVIOLI (BUHARDA MANTI)***** (TURKMENISTAN)

INGREDIENTS

Dough:

2 c water

5 c flour

1 tsp salt

1 egg (optional)

Filling:

1 lb ground beef

2 medium potatoes (chopped)

1 large onion (chopped)

1 tsp black pepper

1 tbsp salt

1 tsp red chili pepper

***Topping**:*

Yogurt

Black pepper

PREPARATION

Mix all dough ingredients together and make smooth hard dough, adding water or flour if needed. Meanwhile, mix filling ingredients well. Fill a stacked steamer pot halfway with water, cover, and heat over medium heat (Adding a pinch of salt to water will help prevent ravioli from sticking to each other). Separate the dough into 3-4 balls, covering with a damp cloth. Start rolling out the first one to ⅛″ thick. Cut into 4½″ squares and put 1 tbsp of filling in the center of each. Connect two diagonal corners by slightly pinching them together. Repeat the process with the other two corners. At this point the dumpling should look like a square envelope. Now connect two adjacent corners by pinching them together. Repeat the process on the opposite side. You should have tulip like shape. (as pictured). Repeat the process with the other dough balls. Lay the dumplings on the oiled boiling steamer racks, leaving ½″ space in between each manti. Stack the racks in the steamer pot. Steam over medium-high heat for 35-40 minutes. Serve with yogurt and black pepper.

UZBEK PILAF (OZBEK PILAVI)***

INGREDIENTS

2 c rice

Warm water to cover rice

1 tsp salt

2 c water

1 lb beef (diced)

6 tbsp butter

2 large carrots (grated)

2 tsp cumin seeds

Salt to taste

6-7 cloves garlic

PREPARATION

Soak the rice in warm salty water for 15 minutes. Drain and rinse with cold water to remove starch. Boil 2 cups of water and add the meat, boil and simmer for about 30 minutes until meat is tender. Remove meat and reserve broth. Melt the butter in a pan and add meat, carrots, drained rice, cumin seeds, salt, garlic cloves and sauté together over medium heat for 5 minutes. Add broth and cover. When the pilaf starts to boil, lower the heat to a simmer, cover, and cook until water is absorbed. Turn off the heat and let it rest for 15 minutes before serving.

FRESH HERB OMELET (KUKU)** (AZERBAIJAN)

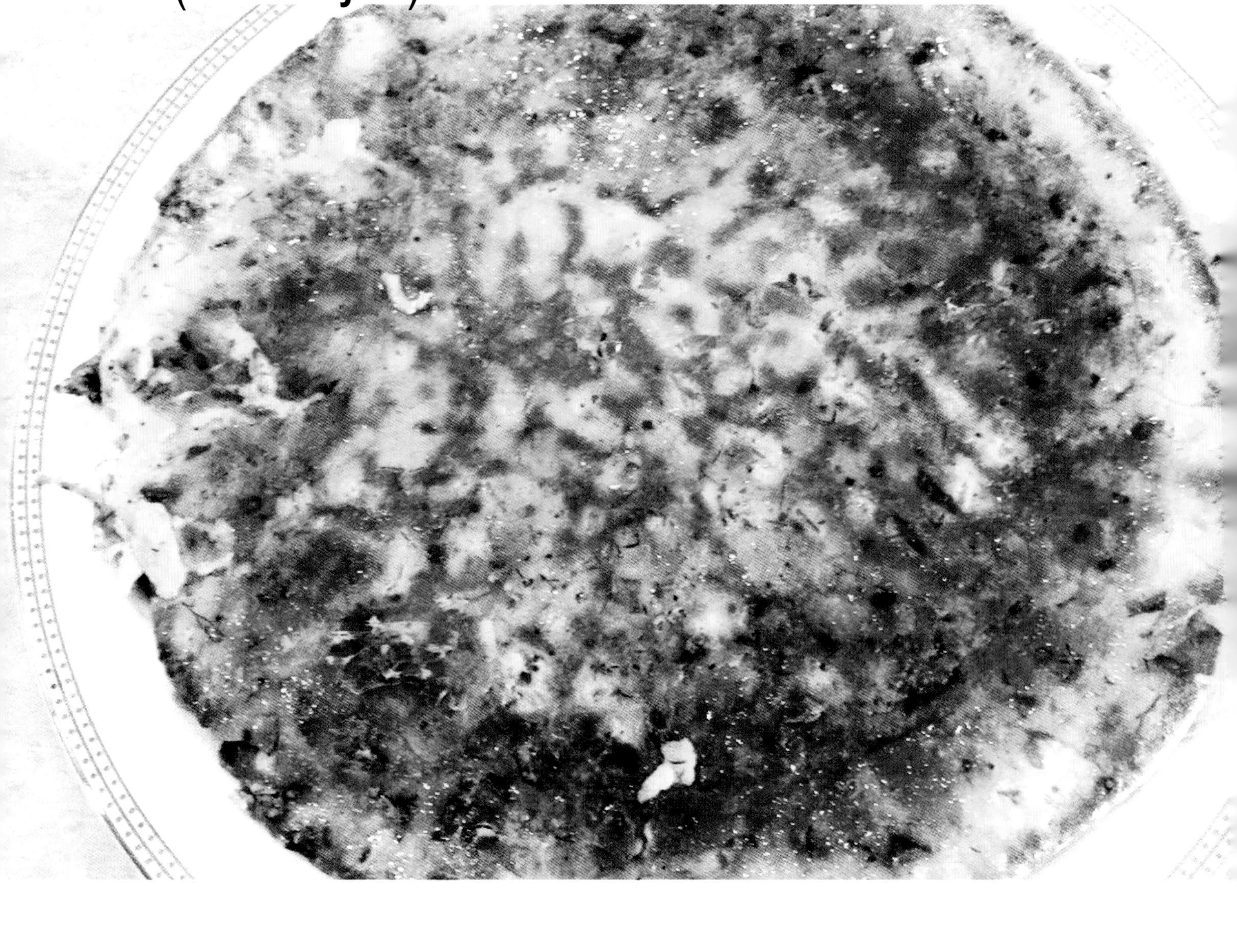

INGREDIENTS

3 c cilantro (chopped)

3 c dill (chopped)

1 c green onions (chopped)

1 c fresh mint (chopped)

1 c spinach (chopped)

8 eggs

Salt and pepper

½ c butter

1 clove minced garlic stirred into 1 c yogurt (optional)

PREPARATION

In a large mixing bowl, combine the chopped fresh herbs and eggs. Add salt and pepper and mix thoroughly. Melt the butter in a medium frying pan over medium heat. Pour the herb-egg mixture into the pan to fill it completely, leveling it with the back of a spoon or by slightly tilting the pan. Lower the heat and cook for about 10 minutes, or until golden brown on the bottom. Using a knife carefully cut the omelet into 4 or more wedges and with the help of a spatula, gently turn them over to brown the other side for another 5-7 minutes. Add more butter if needed. Remove from heat. Transfer the omelet wedges onto a serving platter. Serve immediately with garlicky-yogurt sauce.

ANT HILL COOKIES (KARINCA KULESI KURABIYESI)*** (TURKMENISTAN)

INGREDIENTS

2 eggs

¼ c water

¼ c sugar

1⅔ sticks (½ c plus ⅓ c) butter (room temperature)

4 c flour

½ tsp baking soda

14 oz can sweetened condensed milk

PREPARATION

Preheat oven to 350°F. Mix all ingredients except sweetened condensed milk together. Add flour if needed to make a hard dough. Freeze for one hour before grating into a 9"x13" baking pan. (If dough is not firm enough to grate, freeze a bit longer). Bake grated dough until golden brown. Let the dough crumbs cool and add sweetened condensed milk, mixing thoroughly. Form "ant hills" of the mixture with the help of a small cup or glass. Refrigerate for 20 minutes and serve.

ZEBRA CAKE (AZERBAIJAN)***

INGREDIENTS

4 large eggs (room temperature)

1 c sugar

1 c milk (room temperature)

1 c vegetable oil

½ tsp vanilla

2 c all-purpose flour

1 tbsp baking powder

2 tbsp unsweetened dark cocoa powder

PREPARATION

Preheat the oven to 350°F and grease a 9″x13″ baking pan. In a large mixing bowl, combine eggs and sugar. Using an electric mixer beat until the mixture is creamy and light in color. Add milk, oil, and vanilla and continue beating until well blended. In a separate bowl, mix flour with baking powder. Gradually add the flour mixture to the wet ingredients and beat just until smooth and the dry ingredients are thoroughly incorporated. Divide the mixture into 2 equal portions. Keep one portion plain. Add cocoa powder to the other and mix well. Set out two ¼ c measuring cups. Scoop ¼ c of plain batter into the middle of the baking pan. Then scoop ¼ c of the chocolate batter and pour it on top of the plain batter. Continue with the rest of the batter, first plain and then chocolate to obtain the zebra pattern. Bake for about 35-40 minutes or until an inserted toothpick comes out clean.

KAYMACINA CUSTARD (BOSNIA)**

PREPARATION

Preheat oven to 375°F. Beat eggs with sugar for 5 minutes. Add the milk to the egg-sugar mixture and beat for 3 more minutes. Pour the mixture in a 8″x8″ glass baking pan. Bake in a water bath for about an hour until browned on top. Cool and refrigerate overnight before serving. To serve you may turn one piece upside down on a serving plate and garnish with caramel sauce.

SIDE DISHES

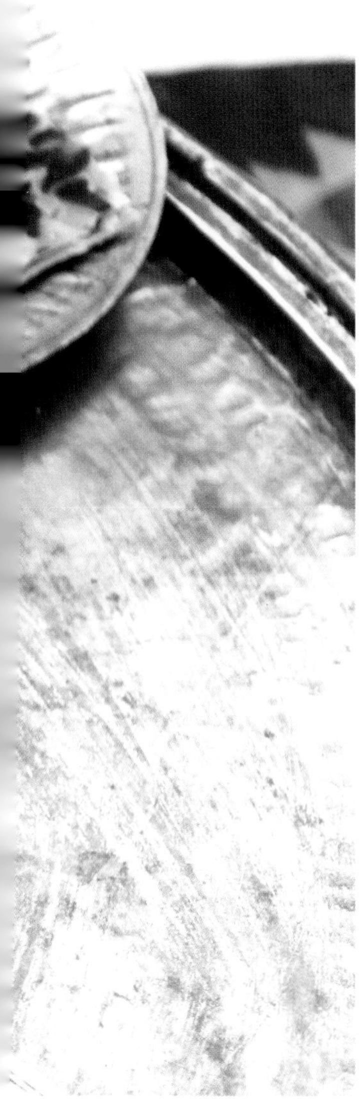

Bulghur

Bulghur is made by cleaning, parboiling, drying, and milling wheat. It's classified according to size. Bulghur is rich in protein, vitamins, minerals, diet sediment fiber, and unsaturated fat. Since a only small portion of the bran is partially removed during processing, it is considered a whole grain. It is commonly confused with cracked wheat which is simply wheat that has been crushed.

Benefits of bulghur: Bulghur is beneficial for the digestive system and has a significant role in weight control as it helps one feel full. According to the World Health Organization, our daily fiber need is around 25-30 grams. We can easily meet this need with one serving of bulghur.

Moreover, it offers a variety as it can be used in dishes ranging from salads to hot and cold entrees. Size of bulghur. The smallest size (#1) is used to make chi-kofte, medium size bulghur (#2) is used for fine bulghur salad (Kisir); and the largest size (#3) is for making bulghur pilaf.

Isot Pepper

Isot pepper is a sun-dried Turkish pepper cultivated in the Urfa province of Turkey. It is red to dark maroon in color and has a smoky, raisin-like taste. It is less spicy than many other chili peppers but provides a more lasting heat. Traditionally in Turkey, it is used in meat and savory dishes. You may find isot pepper online or in Mediterranean or Turkish stores.

Pomegranate sour sauce: Pomegranate sour sauce is prepared using pomegranate juice, syrup or molasses, and pomegranate seeds. Commonly used instead of lemon juice to add tartness todishes,it tastes more sour than sweet. It can also be used to marinate meats or in a salad dressing.

FRIED CAULIFLOWER (KARNABAHAR KIZARTMASI)**

INGREDIENTS

1 head cauliflower, separated into florets

4 c hot water

¼ tsp salt

3 eggs

1 c flour

1 c oil for frying

PREPARATION

Gently boil cauliflower florets in salted water for 5-7 min, being careful not to over boil or the florets will separate. (Tip: If you don't like the smell of cooking cauliflower, add a lemon wedge or 1 tbsp of lemon juice to the cooking water.) Remove from heat and drain. Place 3 eggs into a small bowl. Stir in flour to form a thick batter. Add salt. Heat about 2 inches vegetable oil in a deep sauce pan. Place a few of the tender cauliflower florets in the thick batter and completely coat. Drop one at a time into the hot frying oil. Try to keep the florets separated so they do not stick to each other. Stir occasionally, cooking until golden-brown. Drain on paper towels and serve hot.

ROASTED VEGETABLES (FIRINDA SEBZELER)**

INGREDIENTS

3 zucchinis

5 carrots

1 tbsp olive oil

Salt (divided use)

1 c yogurt

1 clove garlic (minced)

PREPARATION

Preheat oven to 350. Peel zucchini and carrots and slice diagonally at a 45-degree angle. Mix with olive oil and place on an aluminum foil lined baking sheet. Sprinkle with salt and roast 30-45 minutes until vegetables soften, stirring occasionally. Mix garlic, yogurt and salt to taste and pour onto the roasted vegetables.

LENTIL PATTIES (MERCIMEK KOFTESI)***

INGREDIENTS

2 c red lentil

4 c water

1 c fine bulghur (#2)

1 medium onion (chopped)

½ c olive oil

1 tbsp tomato paste

2 tbsp pepper paste

Salt, pepper, and crushed red pepper flakes to taste

4-5 green onions (chopped)

1 c fresh parsley (chopped)

Lettuce leaves (optional, for serving)

PREPARATION

Place red lentils in a large saucepan with the water and cook on low heat. When the lentils have almost absorbed the water, stir in bulghur, cover, and turn off the heat. Let it sit for 15-20 minutes until the bulghur gets very soft. In a small frying pan, sauté onion in olive oil over medium-low heat. Stir in tomato paste, pepper paste, salt, pepper, and crushed red pepper flakes and sauté for 1 minute. Remove from the heat and cool before adding to the bulghur-lentil mixture and knead well. Then gently mix in chopped green onions and parsley. Take walnut size pieces of the mixture and form into oblong shapes. You can serve room temperature lentil patties on lettuce leaves.

POTATO PIZZA (PATATES PIZZASI)**

INGREDIENTS

1 onion (chopped)

1 red bell pepper (diced)

1 yellow or orange bell pepper (diced)

1 green bell pepper (diced)

1 c sausages (diced)

1 c beef hot dogs (cubed)

2 tbsp olive oil

1 tsp salt

¼ tsp pepper to taste

¼ tsp chili powder

1 c mozzarella cheese (grated)

PREPARATION

Preheat oven to 400°F. Sauté onion in olive oil. Add potatoes, salt, peper and chili powder.. After 10 minutes, add bell peppers, sausages and hot dogs. Cook until potatoes are tender, stirring occasionally. Put in a 9" baking dish, spread mozzarella on top and bake until cheese melts.

ZUCCHINI FRITTERS (KABAK MUCVER)**

INGREDIENTS

4 zucchinis, (approximately 4 cups, grated)

3 eggs

⅓ c fresh dill (chopped)

3-4 green onions (finely chopped)

1 c feta cheese

½ tsp salt

¼ tsp black pepper

1 c flour

½ c olive oil for frying

PREPARATION

Put grated zucchini in a colander. Place the zucchini in a bowl. Mix in all the ingredients except flour and oil. Add flour in slowly and mix well. The consistency should be a little thicker than cake batter. Heat oil in a frying pan. Over medium heat, drop 1 ladle of batter into hot oil, a total of 6-7 mounds in the pan. Fry, turning once, until golden-brown, for about 4 minutes on each side. Drain excess oil by placing fritters on paper towels. You may fry the fritters on a griddle.

POTATO PATTIES (PATATES KOFTESI)***

INGREDIENTS

2 c fine bulghur (#2)

2 c hot water

4 potatoes

⅓ c corn oil or olive oil

1 onion (diced)

2 tbsp tomato paste

1 tbsp pepper paste

1 tsp dried mint

½ bunch parsley (chopped)

1 tsp salt

1 tsp chili powder

Juice of ½ lemon

Pomegranate sour sauce (salad dressing) or sumac (both optional)

PREPARATION

Put bulghur in a large bowl with 2 cups of hot water, cover, and let it absorb the water. Boil potatoes until tender. Peel and grate cooked potatoes into bowl with bulghur. Heat oil; add onion; and sauté until lightly browned. Stir in tomato paste and pepper paste. Add to the bulghur and potato mixture and knead until well blended. Add dried mint, chopped parsley, salt, chili powder, and lemon juice (and optional pomegranate sour sauce or sumac if you wish). Mix well and form into golf ball size ovals with your hands. You can serve warm, cold, or at room temperature, on lettuce leaves if you wish.

SCRAMBLED EGG WITH VEGETABLES (MENEMEN)**

INGREDIENTS

1 tbsp olive oil

1 onion (chopped)

2 green peppers (diced)

2 big tomatoes (peeled and diced)

2 eggs

½ tsp salt

PREPARATION

Heat olive oil in a pan. Add onion and sauté until golden. Add green peppers, tomatoes and sauté until the vegetables are tender. Whisk eggs and salt in a bowl and add it to the pan. Lower the heat and cook menemen until the eggs are done. Serve hot for breakfast.

CHI-KOFTE (CIG KOFTE)*****

INGREDIENTS

2 c fine bulghur (#1)

2 tbsp tomato paste

1 tbsp red pepper paste

1½ tsp crushed red pepper

1½ tsp isot (optional)

1½ tsp ground cumin

1 tsp salt

1½ tsp dried mint

1 small onion (finely chopped)

3 cloves of garlic (finely chopped)

1 c hot water

1 c parsley (chopped)

5 green onions (chopped)

1 c olive oil

3 eggs

pinch of salt

1 tsp lemon juice

1 bunch Romaine lettuce or Lavash bread

PREPARATION

Place the bulghur into a large bowl. Add tomato paste, red pepper paste and all the seasonings. Add chopped onion and garlic, knead them all together. Add 1 cup of hot water and continue to knead until the wheat gets tender. (Stir with a spoon to cool.) Heat the oil in a deep nonstick pan. Whisk the eggs with a pinch of salt and cook the eggs in the oil. Add egg-oil mixture and lemon juice to the bulghur mixture. Mix everything first with a spoon and then by kneading. Add parsley and green onions and continue kneading gently. Grab at least walnut size amounts of the mixture, roll into a log, and squeeze and press with your fingers to obtain the appearance as in the picture. Serve them with lettuce or lavash bread.

STUFFED MEATBALL (ICLI KOFTE)*****

INGREDIENTS

Dough:

2 c fine bulghur (#1)
1 c semolina
1 tbsp salt
3 c hot water
1 tbsp tomato paste
1½ tsp red pepper paste
2 eggs
2 tbsp flour
1 tbsp cornstarch

Filling:

3 medium potatoes (peeled)
1 lb ground beef
Scant ½ c vegetable oil
2 medium onions (grated)
1 tsp salt
1 tsp red pepper flakes
¼ tsp black pepper
⅔ c walnut (chopped)

To boil:

5 c water
1 tsp salt
2 tbsp vegetable oil

Topping:

½ c butter

PREPARATION

Place bulghur and semolina in a big bowl. Add salt and water, stir, cover, and allow to soak for 5-10 minutes. After all water is absorbed, add tomato paste, red pepper paste, egg, flour, and cornstarch, then mix well by squeezing with your hands. Let sit for about 10 minutes.

Boil peeled potatoes, cool, and grate. Cook the ground beef and oil in a pan. Add onions and cook for about 6-7 minutes more. Add grated potatoes, spices, and walnut to the ground beef mixture, and mix completely.

Take walnut size amounts of the bulghur mixture and make a well in the middle with your thumb. Make the well bigger while turning in your hand (like you would make a vase on a potter's wheel). The end product should look like a small bell pepper that's ready to stuff. You may wet your finger to make this process easier. Place some filling inside and gently squeeze the meatball closed. Repeat until the bulghur and filling are gone.

Boil water, salt and oil in a pot. Add meatballs and boil gently for 7-8 minutes. When they start to float, they are done; take them out of water with a strainer. Melt butter, pour it over the meatballs, and serve them hot.

YOGURT WITH CUCUMBERS (CACIK)*

INGREDIENTS

1 clove garlic (minced with salt)

1½ c plain yogurt

1 c cucumber (diced)

3 tsp olive oil

Pinch of dried mint

Water (if needed)

PREPARATION

Place the garlic and yogurt in a medium sized bowl. Mix with a wooden spoon until it is blended very well. Add diced cucumber and mix again and add water if needed. With a ladle, pour into small bowls and then add 1 tbsp of olive oil on top of each. Garnish with dried mint.

LEEKS AND CARROTS (HAVUCLU PIRASA)***

INGREDIENTS

1 lb leeks (cleaned carefully to remove sand)

3 carrots (peeled)

1 onion, chopped

½ c olive oil

3 tomatoes (grated)

2 tbsp rice (rinsed to remove starch)

2 tsp sugar

Salt to taste

Juice of ½ lemon

1 c water

PREPARATION

Slice leeks and carrots on the diagonal. Sauté with onions in olive oil. Add grated tomatoes. Add rice, sugar, salt, lemon juice and water. Bring to a boil then reduce heat to simmer. Cook over low heat until tender.

STUFFED ARTICHOKES (ZEYTINYAGLI ENGINAR)***

INGREDIENTS

5-6 artichoke bottoms

4 c water

3 tbsp lemon juice (divided use)

2 tsp salt (divided use)

1 tsp black pepper

2 potatoes, peeled and rinse

15 oz can of carrots (drained)

15 oz can of peas (drained)

½ c onion (chopped)

¼ c olive oil

Dill for decoration (chopped)

PREPARATION

Wash artichoke bottoms and bring 2 c water to a boil with 1 tsp salt and 1 tbsp lemon juice. Add artichoke bottoms and cook until tender. Remove artichokes to ice water. Diced the potatoes. Boil the potatoes in the 2 cups of water until potatoes get tender and drain. Put the olive oil in a pan and add the chopped onion. Sauté onion until the lightly brown. To make stuffing mix, put onion, potatoes, carrots and peas in a big bowl. Add 1 tsp salt, 2 tbsp lemon juice, black pepper and mix well. Put artichokes in the serving dish. Fill the artichoke with stuffing mix. Decorate with the dill.

TURKISH GREEN BEANS (TAZE FASULYE)***

INGREDIENTS

1 pound fresh or frozen (Italian cut) green beans

½ c olive oil

1 medium onion (finely chopped)

2 large tomatoes (peeled, finely chopped)

¼ tsp sugar

Salt to taste

PREPARATION

If you're using fresh green beans, clean and trim them to 1"-1½" pieces. Put olive oil in a pan and add the beans, chopped onions and tomatoes. Add the sugar and salt. Cover and cook over low heat until the beans are soft (30 minutes for frozen beans, 45 minutes for fresh). If you wish to make in a pressure cooker, add everything cook for 15 minutes on medium. This is traditionally served at room temperature, but it's also good when it's warm.

KIDNEY BEANS (ZEYTINYAGLI BARBUNYA)***

INGREDIENTS

1 medium onion (chopped)

2 garlic cloves (chopped)

2 carrots (cut to size of kidney beans)

¼ c olive oil

2 medium potatoes (cut to size of kidney beans)

29 oz can red kidney bean (drained and rinsed)

Salt to taste

3/2 c water

PREPARATION

Sauté onion, garlic and carrots in oil until tender, adding water. Add potatoes, beans and salt. Bring to a boil, reduce heat to simmer and cook until tender.

BLACK-EYED PEAS WITH OLIVE OIL (ZEYTINYAGLI BORULCE)***

INGREDIENTS

2 lb black-eyed peas (frozen)

1 medium onion

4 bell peppers (1 green, 1 red, 1 orange and 1 yellow)

3 tomatoes

2 medium carrots

Scant ½ c extra virgin olive oil

1 c hot water

1 tsp salt

Yogurt to serve

PREPARATION

Boil the black-eyed peas for 20 minutes, drain, and return them to the cooking pot. Slice onion into circles and set them on top. Chop the peppers, tomatoes and carrots and add them to the pan in that order. Add olive oil and water. Bring to a boil, lower the heat, and simmer without stirring until cooked thoroughly. Add salt while still warm, cool, and serve with yogurt.

STUFFED MINI BELL PEPPERS (BIBER DOLMASI)****

INGREDIENTS

4 lb mini bell peppers

1½ c rice

1 medium onion (chopped)

2 tbsp olive oil

1 tbsp tomato paste

1 tbsp pepper paste

Salt, black pepper, cumin, red pepper, dry mint to taste

½ c water

PREPARATION

Preheat oven to 400°F. Rinse and drain the rice. Place onions, oil, rice, tomato paste, pepper paste and spices in a pan. Add ½ cup water and sauté. Cut off the top of the mini bell peppers and remove all seeds. Stuff the peppers ⅔ full with rice mixture. Place in a medium glass baking dish and add 1 c water. Cover with aluminum foil to seal the pan so the peppers steam. Bake for 15 minutes. Remove aluminum foil and continue baking 10 more minutes.

STUFFED GRAPE LEAVES (YAPRAK SARMASI)****

INGREDIENTS

16 oz canned grape leaves

1 medium onion (chopped)

1 tsp tomato paste

1 tsp red pepper paste

2 c Calrose rice

Salt, pepper to taste

1 tbsp dried mint

3 c water (divided use)

3 tbsp olive oil

Rinse well the grape leaves. Sauté onions in a pot and add tomato paste, red pepper paste, rice, salt and dried mint. Then add 1 cup water and cook 7-8 minutes on low heat and cool. Lay a leaf with the stem towards you on a flat surface. The bottom of the leaf should be facing up (the bottom of the leaves are lighter in color and veins of the leaf are more visible there). Place a tablespoon of filling just above the stem and make a ½ an inch thick horizontal line with the filling. Make sure to leave at least 1 inch space from 2 sides. Cut out the stem of the leaf. Fold the sides towards the center. Tightly roll the leave starting from the stem side towards the end. Repeat with the rest of the leaves. Place the rolls in tight layers in the saucepan. Be sure to place the packets with the seam on the bottom. Add 2 cups of water. Place a porcelain plate upside down on the top of the rolls to prevent unrolling. Bring to a boil, and reduce heat to a simmer. Cook about 45 minutes, until the leaves are tender.

CABBAGE STEW (KAPUSKA)***

INGREDIENTS

¼ c olive oil

1 onion (chopped)

3 tbsp tomato paste

1 medium cabbage (sliced)

1 medium potato (diced)

1 tsp salt

1 tsp sugar

4 c hot water

PREPARATION

Heat olive oil in a pot; add onion and sauté until golden. Add tomato paste and sauté for 3 minutes. Then add sliced cabbage to pan, stir for 2 minutes. Add potatoes to pan with salt and sugar. Cook over medium heat for another 5 minutes, stirring from time to time. Finally, add hot water and cook for 25-30 minutes at low heat , bring to a boil, lower heat to a simmer, and cook until potatoes are tender.

SEASONS SALAD (MEVSIM SALATASI)**

INGREDIENTS

Salad:

1 small head romaine lettuce

1 small head red lettuce

1 bunch arugula

1 bunch pepper grass

Leaves from 4-5 stems parsley

1 carrot (grated)

1 medium turnip sliced 15 oz can corn, draine

1 c chopped red cabbage

6-7 cherry tomatoes

1-2 fresh mint leaves

1-2 purple basil leaves

Dressing:

¼ c plus 2 tbsp olive oil

Salt to taste

1 lemon juice

2 tbsp apple cider vinegar (for red cabbage)

PREPARATION

Clean all salad ingredients, cut, and put in a deep bowl. Add olive oil, salt and lemon juice,and vinegar mix well and serve.

POTATO SALAD (PATATES SALATASI)**

INGREDIENTS

5 potatoes (medium)

1 onion

5 tbsp olive oil

Juice of 2 lemons

Salt and pepper to taste

4-5 leaves romaine lettuce (chopped)

1 c chopped parsley

PREPARATION

Boil the potatoes and drain. In the meantime, peel onion and cut into half-moons. Put the sliced onion in a bowl and rub with salt until soft. Rinse and drain onion. To make the dressing, mix oil and lemon juice together and season to taste with salt and black pepper. While still warm but cool enough to touch, peel the boiled potatoes and cut them in medium sized chunks. Add half of the dressing to the potatoes while they are still warm. After the potatoes cool, add the rest of the dressing. Add onion, lettuce and chopped parsley, mix well.

BLACK-EYED PEA SALAD (BORULCE SALATASI)**

INGREDIENTS

2-15 oz cans black-eyed peas

1 bunch parsley (chopped)

3 green onions (chopped)

1 c walnut (chopped)

1½ tbsp olive oil

Scant ¼ c pomegranate sour sauce (or lemon juice)

Salt and pepper to taste

PREPARATION

Drain and rinse black-eyed peas and place in a large bowl. Add the rest of the ingredients. Mix well and refrigerate for at least 1 hour before serving.

BEAN SALAD (PIYAZ)**

INGREDIENTS

15 oz can navy beans

¼ c onion (sliced)

¼ tsp salt to soften onion

Salt to taste

1 c parsley (chopped)

2 tbsp olive oil

Juice of ½ lemon

PREPARATION

Drain and rinse the beans. Knead sliced onions with salt, rinse, and drain. Mix beans with onions and parsley. Toss with olive oil and lemon juice. Optionally, sliced hard boiled egg, olives, tomato, or similar ingredients can be added according to your taste.

PURSLANE SALAD (SEMIZOTU SALATASI)**

INGREDIENTS

4 potatoes

8 oz jar pickles, drained

8 oz jar pimento-stuffed green olives, drained

1 bunch purslane

8 oz canned corn, drained

Dressing:

3 tbsp yogurt

2 tbsp olive oil

1 tbsp mayonnaise

1 tsp mustard

1 tsp salt

1 tsp dried mint

PREPARATION

Boil the potatoes. Peel and cube the potatoes. Thinly slice the pickles and green olives and chop the purslane. Put all in a bowl with the corn and mix. Blend dressing ingredients and toss with the salad just before serving.

FINE BULGHUR SALAD (KISIR)***

PREPARATION

Put the bulghur in a bowl, pour hot water over, cover, and let the bulghur absorb the water.Sauté the onion with olive oil, and stir in tomato and red pepper pastes. Cool and add to the bulghur. Add spices to lemon juice, mix well and add to bulghur mixture. Add green onion and parsley to the bulghur mixture. You may decorate with pickles, lettuce, and tomatoes on the side as a garnish.

INGREDIENTS

2 c fine bulghur (#1)

2 c hot water

1 onion (finely chopped)

5 tbsp olive oil

1 tbsp tomato paste

1 tbsp red pepper paste

Ground black pepper, crushed red pepper, and salt to taste

2 tbsp lemon juice 5 green onions (sliced)

½ bunch parsley (chopped)

Romaine lettuce,

pickles, and tomatoes (optional)

2 tomatoes

5 pickles(small Persian)

GREEN LENTIL SALAD (YESIL MERCIMEK SALATASI)***

INGREDIENTS

2 c green lentils

Juice of 2-3 lemons (divided use)

Salt to taste

1 yellow bell pepper (chopped)

1 green bell pepper (chopped)

1 red bell pepper (chopped)

4 green onions (chopped)

½ c dill pickles (finely chopped)

½ c fresh dill (chopped

1 tbsp extra-virgin Olive oil

½ c parsley (chopped)

½ c walnuts (finely chopped)

PREPARATION

Rinse and drain the lentils. Put in a pot, cover with water by 3 inches, and bring to a boil. Turn down to a simmer and cook until tender (adding more water if necessary), about 30 minutes, and drain. Mix drained lentils with the juice of 2 lemons, salt, all the vegetables, and cucumbers and pickles.. Let them sit for 5 minutes. Taste and add more salt and lemon juice if needed. Add the extra-virgin olive oil, parsley, dill, and walnuts. Stir to combine.

MUSHROOM SALAD (MANTAR SALATASI)**

INGREDIENTS

14 oz can sliced mushrooms

7-8 pickles (small Persian)

1 c parsley (chopped)

10-12 pimento-stuffed green olives

3 tbsp canned or boiled fresh sweet corn

1 Lemon juice

1 tbsp Olive oil

Salt to taste

PREPARATION

Drain and rinse mushrooms. Put in a bowl. Cut the pickles, parsley and the olives in small pieces. Add to the bowl along with the corn and mix well. Finally, add the lemon juice, oil and salt. Toss and serve the salad immediately.

ONION TOMATO SALAD (SOGANLI DOMATES SALATASI)*

INGREDIENTS

1 onion

½ c parsley (chopped)

Salt, sumac to taste

2 tomatoes

PREPARATION

Quarter the onion and slice thinly, gently rub with some salt, rinse and drain. Mix onion with parsley, salt, and sumac. Plate the onion salad and serve with sliced tomatoes.

CARROT-ZUCCHINI SALAD (HAVUC-KABAK SALATASI)**

INGREDIENTS

2 large zucchinis

2 medium carrots

¼ c yogurt

2 tbsp mayonnaise

½ c dill (chopped)

2 cloves garlic

½ c walnuts (coarsely ground)

PREPARATION

Grate zucchini and carrots; sauté them until tender. Whisk other ingredients together then stir in the warmed zucchini-carrot mixture. This salad can also be served cold.

ROASTED EGGPLANT SALAD (HERSE)***

INGREDIENTS

2 large eggplants (about 2 lb total)

2 green bell peppers

2 red bell peppers

2 tomatoes

½ c parsley (finely chopped)

1-2 cloves garlic (minced)

Salt to taste

Lemon juice to taste

2 tbsp olive oil

PREPARATION

Lay aluminum foil on the oven rack, rinse the eggplants and bell peppers and pierce with a fork. Bake them on high broil preheat oven 500°F and put under the broiler turning occasionally until they are completely wrinkled and the skin is charred. Remove from oven and place in a covered bowl to cool. (The steam will make them easier to peel.) Peel and remove seeds from the bell peppers. Dice the tomatoes and roasted vegetables; add parsley, garlic, salt, lemon juice and olive oil. Mix well, slightly crushing the roasted vegetables.

RED BEET SALAD (KIRMIZI PANCAR SALATASI)*

INGREDIENTS

2 medium beets

2 cloves garlic

¼ c plus 2 tbsp yogurt

2 tbsp mayonnaise

Salt to taste

PREPARATION

Boil the beets, cool, peel, and shred into a large bowl. Stir in minced garlic, yogurt, mayonnaise, and salt.

PILAF (PILAV)**

INGREDIENTS

2 c long grain rice

3 tbsp butter

2½ tsp salt (divided use)

2½ c boiling water

PREPARATION

Soak the rice for 15 minutes in warm water with 1 tsp of salt. Drain and rinse with cold water to remove the starch. Drain completely. Melt the butter in a pan and add rice, stirring continuously. Sprinkle with remaining 1½ tsp salt. Add 2½ cups boiling water, return to a boil, lower the heat, and cook until the water boils away. Turn off the heat and cover. Let the pilaf stand covered for about 15 minutes before serving.

VARIATION I: PILAF WITH ORZO (ARPA SEHRIYELI PILAV)**

INGREDIENTS

Pilaf recipe ingredients

½ cup orzo

1 tbsp oil

PREPARATION

Heat the oil in a pan and cook the orzo until brown, stirring continuously. Add the butter and rice and continue stirring. Continue as in pilaf recipe.

VARIATION 2: PILAF WITH TOMATOES (DOMATESLI PILAV)**

INGREDIENTS

Pilaf recipe ingredients

2 big size tomatoes (chopped)

PREPARATION

Sauté chopped tomatoes in melted butter. Add soaked, rinsed and drained rice and sauté for 2 minutes more. Continue as in pilaf recipe.

VARIATION 3: CYPRUS PILAF (KIBRIS PILAVI)***

INGREDIENTS

Pilaf recipe ingredients (Use ½ c olive oil instead of butter)

1 c red cabbage (chopped thinly)

1 carrot (shredded)

3-4 green onions (chopped)

½ bunch parsley (chopped)

½ bunch dill (chopped)

1 tsp vinegar

Juice of ½ lemon

PREPARATION

Cook and cool the rice pilaf according the pilaf recipe. Mix carrot, red cabbage, parsley, green onion, dill, vinegar, salt, lemon juice, and add to the cooked rice.

BULGHUR PILAF (BULGUR PILAVI) **

INGREDIENTS

1 large onion (chopped)

2 tsp olive oil

1 tbsp tomato paste

1 tbsp pepper paste

2 c bulghur (#3)

Salt to taste

1 tsp dried mint

1 tsp Crushed red pepper

2 c hot water

PREPARATION

Sauté chopped onion in olive oil until golden. Stir in tomato paste and pepper paste . Add bulghur, salt, mint, crushed red pepper and stir 2-3 more minutes. Add hot water and bring to a boil. Cover and lower the heat, cooking until the bulghur absorbs all of the water. Remove from heat and let pilaf stand for at least 10 minutes before serving.

VARIATION I: BULGHUR PILAF WITH SUN DRIED TOMATOES (KURU DOMATESLI BULGUR PILAVI)

INGREDIENTS

½ c sun dried tomatoes (petite, finely diced)

Warm water to cover

Bulghur pilaf ingredients

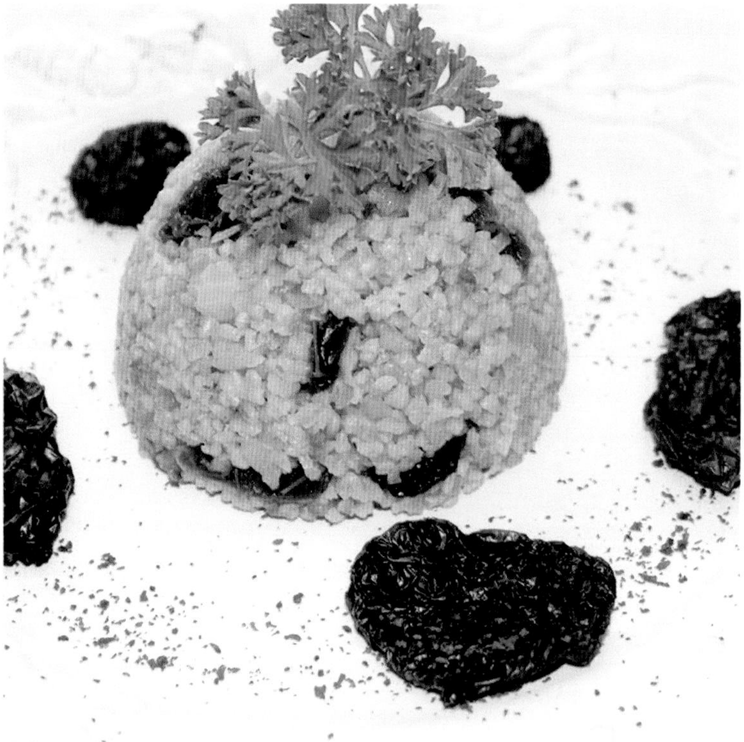

PREPARATION

Soak sun dried tomatoes in warm water for 15-20 minutes. Drain. Add to the pot at the same time as the bulghur and continue as the bulghur pilaf recipe directs.

VARIATION 2: BULGHUR PILAF WITH GREEN LENTILS (YESIL MERCIMEKLI BULGUR PILAVI)***

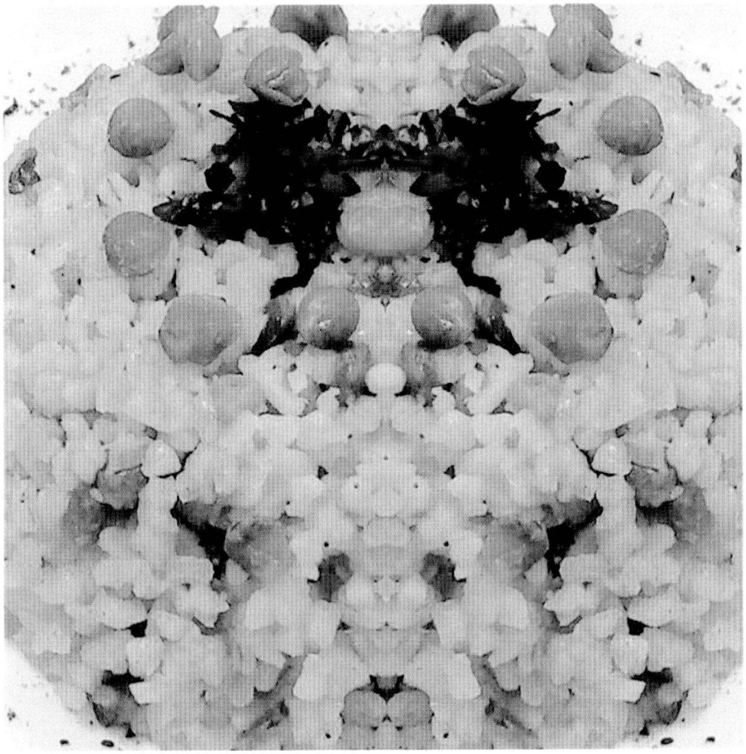

INGREDIENTS

½ c green lentils

2 c bulghur (#3)

2 tbsp butter

2-3 tbsp oil

1 onion (chopped)

3 c hot water

Salt and pepper to taste

PREPARATION

Boil green lentils for 5 min and drain, reserving cooking liquid for use later in the recipe if desired. Put butter and oil in another pan over medium heat and stir. Add onion and continue stirring while cooking. Add rinsed bulghur, slightly boiled lentils, 3 cups hot water (and/or reserved lentil cooking liquid), salt and black pepper. Bring to a boil, cover, and reduce heat to a simmer. Cook until tender,and until the absorbs all of the water and serve hot.

ORZO PILAF (SEHRIYE PILAVI)**

INGREDIENTS

2 tbsp butter

1 tbsp olive oil

2 c orzo

4 c hot water

Salt to taste

PREPARATION

Melt butter over medium heat in a non-stick pan. When butter starts to bubble, add olive oil and orzo. Cook, stirring constantly, until orzo is lightly browned. Add hot water and salt. Bring to a boil, cover, and reduce heat to simmer. Cook the orzo until it absorbs all the liquid and then turn off the heat. Let the pilaf stand off the burner. at least 10-15 minutes before serving.

COUSCOUS PILAF (KUSKUS PILAVI)*

INGREDIENTS

8 c water

2 tsp salt (divided use)

1 tbsp corn oil

16 oz package pearl couscous (also called Israeli couscous)

¼ cup butter

PREPARATION

Put water, 1 tsp salt and oil in a deep pot and bring to a boil. Add couscous and boil for 15 minutes, stirring occasionally. Drain. Melt butter in the pot and return couscous to the pot. Stir in 1 tsp salt, cook over medium heat for 2 minutes and serve.

HOME MADE NOODLE (ERISTE)*****

INGREDIENTS

3 eggs

3 c flour (If needed you may add more flour to get a hard dough)

⅔ c water

Salt to taste

PREPARATION

Knead all ingredients together, separate dough into 2 pieces and let them rest for 30 minutes. Roll each out until they are paper thin and let rest for 15 to 20 minutes. Sprinkle with flour and slice into 2" strips. Stack the strips 4 or 5 layers high and cut them into ¼"-½"pieces. Sprinkle these with flour and let them rest and dry for about a day.

These noodles can be made in advance and dried or boiled fresh. These dried eriste noodles can be stored in airtight containers and frozen for up to 9 months. To cook frozen noodles, thaw them first. Then add 1 tbsp of salt and 2 tbsp of butter into a pot with water and bring to a boil. Stir in the thawed noodles and continue boiling for 8-10 minutes with the lid half covered. Drain, rinse under cold running water briefly, drain again and serve immediately.

NOTE: (This recipe is prepared over two days)

PASTRIES

PASTRIES

Pastries are one of the most important parts of the traditional Turkish dinner table. They are served as warm appetizers. Although there are sweet ones, in Turkish Cuisine, pastries are mostly savory. In this section you will be introduced to many delightful traditional Turkish pastries.

The main components of Turkish pastries are:

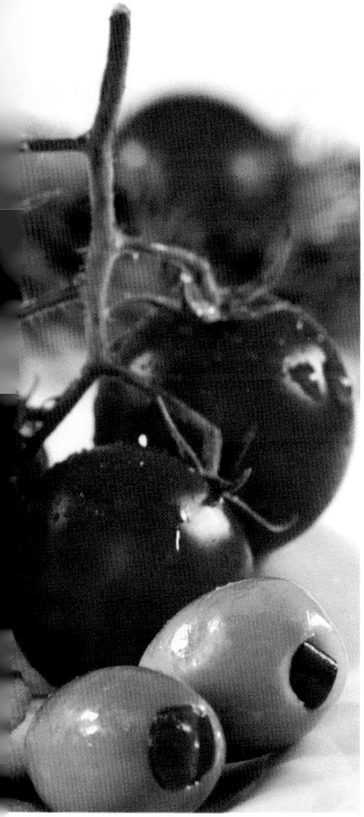

Turkish Phyllo Dough (*Yufka*): Most Turkish pastries call for Turkish phyllo dough, a commercially available thin, round, dough. Some women prefer to use home made phyllo dough as well. It is made with flour, water and salt. The phyllo itself can be folded, rolled up or layered. There are two different sizes of phyllo dough used in these recipes: Paper-thin phyllo dough (which is used for making baklava, Athens brand phyllo dough size #4) or regular thickness (Athens brand size #8). The filling could be cheese, beef, chicken, pastrami, sausage, vegetables, or herbs. When working with phyllo dough, do not open the package until you are ready to use it, and then cover with a damp cloth to prevent it from drying out. If your dough is frozen, it's best to defrost it in the refrigerator.

Turkish Rolling Pin (*Oklava*): The Turkish rolling pin looks like a very thin, long broomstick, with a diameter of 0.8"-1". The oklava is used to roll out Turkish phyllo dough. If you don't have one, you may use a regular rolling pin.

Black Cumin Seeds: Black cumin (Nigella sativa) belongs to the buttercup family and has black, thick seeds. Black cumin seeds are commonly used as a seasoning in many different cuisines across the world. Interestingly, black cumin seeds contain more that 100 chemical compounds and are believed to have many health benefits. Some of these health benefits are:

- calms nervous system, quells colic pain in babies.
- strengthens immune system
- calms upset stomach, treats flatulence, diarrhea, hemorrhoids, constipation and dysentery.
- stimulates energy and helps in recovery from fatigue and low spirits.
- an effective cure for skin conditions. (from naturalnews.com)

PACANGA PASTRY (PACANGA BOREGI)**

INGREDIENTS

3 pieces of Turkish phyllo dough (yufka)

12 slices Pastrami

1 banana pepper (or green bell pepper) (sliced thinly)

1 tomato (peeled and diced)

6 slices Mozzarella cheese

Oil for frying

PREPARATION

Cut the stack of phyllo into four triangles. Sauté pepper with tomato for 1-2 min and put about 1 tbsp of the mixture on the wide side of 1 triangle phyllo. Top with half a slice of mozzarella and one slice of pastrami and fold the sides of the phyllo in and roll them up tightly. Repeat with the 11 other pieces of phyllo. Heat the oil and deep fry until golden brown. Drain on paper towels and serve hot.

CHEESE PASTRIES WITH OREGANO (KEKIKLI, PEYNIRLI POGACA)****

INGREDIENTS

Dough:

2 tbsp sugar (divided use)

2 tbsp yeast

1 c milk (warm)

3 c flour

1 tsp salt

½ c butter (softened, diced)

3 egg yolks (1 egg yolk separated for top)

Filling:

¾ c crumbled feta cheese

¾ c shredded cheddar cheese

2 tsp freshly grounded black pepper

2 tbsp oregano

PREPARATION

Preheat oven to 375°F and line a sheet cake pan with parchment paper. Melt 2 tbsp sugar and yeast into warm milk and let sit for 10 minutes. Mix dough ingredients; knead until you obtain firm dough. Put the dough into an oiled bowl and let stand for 1½-2 hours at room temperature. (You may also prepare the dough in a bread machine). Roll dough into a 15″×18″ rectangle on a lightly floured counter. Spread with the filling ingredients. Fold dough in half to 15″×9.″ Roll out dough again to 10″×18.″ Cut into 10 inch long and ½″ wide ribbons. Take each from the ends and gently twist. Form each piece of twisted dough into a circle, tucking one end under the other, and place on a baking pan. Be careful that they do not touch one another. Brush the top with beaten egg yolk and bake for about 40 minutes.

CRUNCHY POTATO PASTRIES (CITIR PATATES BOREGI)**

INGREDIENTS

¼ c butter

5-6 medium potatoes (peeled and boiled)

1¼ c feta cheese

2 eggs

½ c milk

½ c yogurt

¼ tsp salt

3 pieces of Turkish phyllo dough (yufka)

PREPARATION

Melt the butter and let it cool. Grate the potatoes and cheese. Mix all the ingredients except the phyllo. Spread out one of the phyllo sheets in a single layer. Spread it with one third of the mixture. Then place one other phyllo sheet on the mixture as a single layer and spread one half of the rest of the mixture. Continue with the last phyllo sheet and spread all the rest of the mixture on top of it. This will make a stack of 3 phyllo dough with a mixture layer within. Fold two opposite edges for 3 inch towards to center, and make a tight roll. Place in a baking dish and cover with greased aluminum foil. Let it rest for 2-3 hours or overnight in the refrigerator. Before baking, place it in the freezer for 30 minutes until firm and easy to slice. Meanwhile, preheat oven to 400°F. Cut the roll into ½" slices and place them on a lightly greased baking pan. Bake until golden brown, about 25 minutes.

PEA QUICHE (BEZELYELI KIS)****

INGREDIENTS

Dough:

1¼ c flour

¾ c butter

½ c water

¼ tsp salt

Vegetables:

1 zucchini

1 bunch green onions

½ c sun dried tomatoes

1 c peas

Cream:

1 c milk

½ c heavy whipping cream

2 eggs

3 tbsp flour

½ tsp salt

¼ tsp white pepper

¼ tsp crushed red pepper

PREPARATION

Preheat the oven 375°F. Mix the dough ingredients and refrigerate for one hour. Then roll the dough out to fit an 8″ deep dish pie plate. Cut the vegetables into small pieces, about the size of the peas, and put them over the crust. Mix the cream filling ingredients and pour on top. Bake the quiche for about 45 minutes. Serve warm.

PASTRY WITH FETA CHEESE AND SPINACH (BEYAZ PEYNIRLI, ISPANAKLI BOREK)***

INGREDIENTS

2-3 c feta cheese

10 oz fresh spinach (washed and drained)

¼ tsp black pepper

1 c milk

½ c extra virgin olive oil

1 c plain yogurt

2 egg yolks

5 pieces of Turkish Phyllo dough

PREPARATION

Preheat the oven 375°F and grease a sheet cake pan. For this dish we need 3 separate bowls. In the first mix feta cheese, spinach and black pepper. In the second mix milk and olive oil. And finally in the third bowl, blend the yogurt and the egg yolks until creamy. Unfold one sheet of pastry. Brush with the milk and oil mixture. Top it with cheese and spinach mixture and gently roll it up securely. Place on a greased baking pan. Repeat this process with the remaining 4 pieces of phyllo dough. Form one spiral using all pieces of rolled dough. Finally brush the top with the yogurt mixture. Bake for about 20-25 minutes until golden brown.

FLAT BREAD WITH SPINACH (GOZLEME)**

INGREDIENTS

1 medium onion (chopped)

1 bag baby spinach (9 oz) (washed, chopped)

Black pepper

Chili powder

½ c feta cheese

15-20 raw tortillas

Butter

PREPARATION

Mix onions with spinach, black pepper, and chili powder. Add feta cheese and mix. Place 1 tbsp spinach mixture on one half of tortilla and fold over to cover the filling. Seal the tortilla by pressing on the edges. If it is too dry, brush the edges with water before sealing. (Note that you can freeze the prepared flat breads and cook them later.) Fry in a nonstick pan over medium heat until both sides are golden brown. Alternatively you can bake them in a 350°F oven for 20-25 minutes. Finally, brush both sides of gozleme with softened butter.

VARIATIONS OF GOZLEME:

YOU CAN ALSO PREPARE THE FLAT BREAD WITH POTATO, CHEESE, OR GROUND BEEF FILLING:

POTATO FILLING:

¼ c olive oil

1 large onion (chopped)

2 tbsp tomato paste

4 medium potatoes (boiled, peeled, and shredded)

¼ tsp black pepper

Salt to taste

PREPARATION

Caramelize the onions in olive oil. Add tomato paste; cook for 5 minutes; and add the potatoes, salt, and black pepper and cook for 5 more minutes. Take the pan off the stove. Let the filling cool for at least 5 minutes. Prepare the flat breads with 1 tablespoon of this filling for each.

GROUND BEEF FILLING:

½ lb ground beef

1 small onion finely chopped

¼ tsp black pepper

Salt to taste

PREPARATION

Mix all ingredients in a bowl. Prepare the flat breads with 1 tablespoon of this filling for each, being careful to spread the raw ground beef thinly so it cooks evenly.

CHEESE FILLING:

2 c feta cheese (crumbled)

1 c finely chopped parsley

PREPARATION

Mix the cheese and the parsley in a bowl. Prepare the flat breads with 1 tablespoon of this filling for each.

ABOUT GOZLEME

Gozleme is originally made from scratch with dough made from flour, water and salt. Each piece of gozleme dough is flattened into a round shape with a rolling pin. The filling is placed in the middle as a square. The sides are folded onto each other to cover the filling. Gozleme is cooked over a small fire covered by a sheet iron like a domed lid. (Sac), brushed with butter on top and served hot usually with a yogurt drink called ayran. You may find gozleme-making tents in almost every tourist part of Turkish cities. The gozlemes are prepared fresh and served immediately.

OLIVE BREAD (ZEYTINLI EKMEK)****

INGREDIENTS

1¾ c water

1½ tsp salt

1 tbsp sugar

3 tbsp butter or margarine

4 c flour

1 tbsp yeast

Filling:

6 oz jar olive paste

2 tbsp tomato paste

2 garlic cloves (minced)

¼ tsp black pepper

¼ tsp chili pepper

1 tsp oregano

Topping:

1 egg yolk

Sesame seeds and black cumin

PREPARATION

Put all bread ingredients into the bread machine and make the dough. If you knead the dough yourself, put a damp cloth over; let it sit for 1 hour to rise after kneading. In another bowl, mix filling ingredients. Preheat the oven 375°F and grease a sheet cake pan. Grease your hands and divide the raised dough into two pieces. Put them onto a clean kitchen counter and gently stretch each of them out with oiled hands. Do not add flour. Evenly spread half of the filling mixture on each. Roll up dough and place on oiled pan. Brush tops with egg yolk and sprinkle with sesame seeds and black cumin. Let dough rise until double in size and bake about 45 minutes. You can serve warm.

TALAS PASTRY (TALAS BOREGI)***

INGREDIENTS

1 lb beef (diced) (entrecote or tenderloin)

2 tbsp oil

1 onion (chopped)

1 tbsp tomato paste

1 tomato (peeled and diced)

1 c diced carrot and 1 c peas (or 1 can mixed carrots and peas (15 oz))

Salt to taste

¼ tsp chili powder

¼ tsp ground black pepper

1 tsp oregano

½ c margarine

¼ c oil

1 package thin phyllo dough (Athens brand #4, for making baklava)

1 egg yolk

Sesame and black cumin seed (to sprinkle on top)

PREPARATION

Put diced beef into a saucepan, cover with water, and boil. Let the water evaporate, stir in oil and onion. Add tomato paste and tomato. Saute for about 30 minutes until meat is tender. Meanwhile, boil carrots and peas, drain, and mix thoroughly with seasonings. If you use the canned veggies no need to boil, but drain and rinse.

Preheat the oven 350°F. Melt margarine and mix with oil. Take one phyllo pastry sheet, spread with the margarine-oil mixture, top with a second phyllo sheet and repeat until you have a stack 4-5 sheets high. Cut stack into four equal rectangles. Put some meat mixture in the middle and fold the sides like an envelope. Place on baking pan, brush with egg yolk, and sprinkle with sesame seeds and black cumin seeds. Bake until golden brown, about 30 minutes.

TURKISH BAGEL (SIMIT)****

INGREDIENTS

(Makes 7 bagels)

3 c flour (plus ½ c extra if needed)

1 tsp salt

1 tsp sugar

1 package instant yeast

1 c water (plus ½ c extra if needed)

Topping:

¼ c molasses

¼ c water

2½ c sesame seeds

PREPARATION

In a deep bowl mix 3 c flour, salt, sugar and yeast. Make a hole in the center and add water. Knead the dough and slowly add up to ½ c of flour to make a soft, smooth dough. Divide the dough into 7 pieces and put a damp cloth over them; let them rise for 30 minutes. Preheat the oven 350°F. Roll each dough ball into a ½" diameter log, fold in half, twist and connect the ends to make a circle. Toast sesame seeds briefly over medium heat until golden and transfer to a plate. Mix molasses with water and dip bagels in it and then in toasted sesame seeds. Put the bagels on a baking pan lined with parchment paper and bake until golden brown, about 30 minutes.

About Turkish Bagels (Simit)

Turkish bagel is a famous street food usually eaten at breakfast with cheese and Turkish black tea. There are several simit houses where you can enjoy fresh simits baked in clay oven. In some parts of the city you will find simit sellers with a small cart or on a round tray on top of their head. Teenage boys selling them will shout out "Who wants hot, crispy simits?" while walking down busy streets.

TURKISH PIZZA (LAHMACUN)**

INGREDIENTS

Topping:

1 onion

1 small bunch parsley

3 Roma tomatoes

2 green peppers

½ lb ground beef

1 tbsp tomato paste

1 tbsp red pepper paste

3 tbsp oil

Salt, pepper

10-11 raw frozen tortillas, thawed

Garnish:

Chopped parsley

Lemon wedges

PREPARATION

Chop onion, parsley, tomatoes and pepper finely using a food processor. Add raw ground beef, tomato paste, red pepper paste, oil, and salt and mix. Spread this filling over the uncooked tortillas in a thin layer; cook covered at low heat in a large nonstick pan. Alternatively, bake in a 450°F oven for 5 minutes.

SALTY CRACKERS (TUZLU KURABIYE)***

INGREDIENTS

4 c flour

1 c margarine at room temperature

1 tablespoon vinegar

1 teaspoon salt

Topping:

1 egg yolk

Sesame seeds

Black cumin

PREPARATION

Preheat oven to 375°F. Line a 9″x13″ baking dish with parchment paper. Mix flour, vinegar, salt and margarine in a bowl and knead well. Place the dough on a flat surface. Roll out to ½″ thick. Cut into 1″x1″ squares or with a cookie cutter. Place the pieces on the baking dish with the help of a spatula. Brush tops with egg yolk and sprinkle with sesame seeds and black cumin. Bake for 15-20 minutes until golden brown. Cool for 15 minutes before serving.

WALNUT ROLLS (CEVIZLI SARMA)****

INGREDIENTS

Dough:

1¾ c water

1½ tsp salt

1 tbsp sugar

3 tbsp butter or margarine

4 c flour

1 tbsp yeast

Filling:

1 c walnuts (chopped)

1 tsp allspice

½ tsp ground cinnamon

1 tbsp sugar

1 egg yolk

1 tsp sesame seeds

PREPARATION

Put dough ingredients in the bread machine and make firm bread dough. Mix chopped walnuts, allspice, cinnamon and sugar. Preheat the oven to 375°F. Divide the dough into two pieces. Press out the dough with oiled hand (like pizza dough). Sprinkle half of walnut mixture onto it, roll up, and cut into 3" pieces. Place them on a greased pan. Brush with beaten egg yolk and sprinkle with sesame seeds. Allow to rise for one hour. Bake until golden brown, about 35 minutes

About Walnut Rolls (Cevizli Lokum)

Walnut rolls are traditionally made at Henna night parties in the Bursa province of Turkey. Walnut rolls are served with mixed nuts as a treat to the guests.

BLACK SEA FLAT BREAD WITH CHEESE (KARADENIZ PIDESI)****

INGREDIENTS

Dough:

1⅓ c water

2 tbsp powdered milk (optional)

1½ tbsp salt

1 tbsp sugar

2 tbsp butter or margarine

3¼ c flour

1 tbsp yeast

Filling:

4 c feta cheese

2 c parsley (chopped)

1 egg

Butter

PREPARATION

Preheat oven to 400°F. Make dough using the dough ingredients. Knead well until it becomes smooth. Cut egg-sized pieces and cover them with a clean damp cloth, put aside for 10 minutes. Crumble feta cheese and mix with chopped parsley. Roll the dough balls into ovals, (about 5"x10." Spread the filling on the each dough leaving 1 inch on the sides empty. Fold the edges over to create a ridged edge and press gently. Beat the egg and brush onto each pide. Bake until golden brown, about 25 minutes. Brush with softened butter after removing from the oven.

About Flat bread from Konya region of Turkey (Etli ekmek)

Flat bread is one of the most famous dishes in the Konya and Sivas regions of Turkey. Main toppings are thinly diced lamb meat, onions, tomatoes and green peppers. Usually people make the topping mix at home and take it to a bakery. The baker will distribute the filling on top of the flattened oval-shaped dough and stretch it with his hands up to 35-40 inches. The flat bread is baked in wood fire oven. Flat bread is very thin, crispy, and not filling. It is commonly served with a yogurt drink (ayran) and salad. Etliekmek is served at weddings as well as birth and circumcision ceremonies

PETITE PIZZA (MINI PIZZA)***

INGREDIENTS

1¼ c canola oil

1¼ c warm water

3 eggs (divided use)

3 tbsp plain yogurt

1½ tbsp instant yeast

3 tbsp sugar

1 tsp salt

Flour (~5 c)

Filling:

2 c grated mozzarella cheese

½ c soujuk, Turkish sausage (sliced)

2 tomatoes (sliced)

PREPARATION

Preheat the oven to 350°F. Line three 9"x13" baking dishes with parchment paper. Separate two eggs, reserving 2 yolks for later use. Whisk the canola oil, warm water, remaining egg, two egg whites, and yogurt in a bowl. Next add yeast, sugar, salt and flour. Make a smooth dough . Take walnut size pieces of dough and roll into balls. Flatten by hand or with a rolling pin to ½" thickness. Place soujuk, tomato slices and mozzarella on top to make little pizzas. Place on a cooking sheet covered with parchment paper and brush with the reserved egg yolks. Bake until golden brown, about 35 minutes.

PASTRY WITH CHEESE (PEYNIRLI POGACA)***

INGREDIENTS

4 tbsp instant yeast

1 tsp sugar

1/2 c warm water

4 c flour

1 c canola oil

1 c plain yogurt

1 tsp salt

2 eggs (divided use)

Filling:

2 c feta cheese (crumbled)

1 c parsley (chopped)

Topping:

Sesame seeds

Black cumin seeds

PREPARATION

Put the yeast and sugar into ½ cup of warm water and mix. Sift the flour and add the canola oil, yogurt, salt and one whole egg and one egg yolk. (Save the other yolk for the egg wash used later.) Add the yeast mixture and knead until you have soft dough. Make golf-ball sized pieces from the dough and flatten them in your hand. Put some of the filling ingredients in the middle and close it so you have a ball shaped pastry with filling.

Place the dough balls on baking pan, about 2" apart. Brush the tops with the reserved egg yolk and sprinkle with sesame seeds or black cumin seeds. Let them rest for 2 hours in a warm place. Preheat oven to 400°F and bake until golden brown, about 35 minutes.

KANDIL SESAME RINGS (KANDIL SIMIDI)***

INGREDIENTS

2 egg yolks

2 tbsp vinegar

½ c corn oil

3 tbsp sugar

1 tsp salt

¾ c butter (room temperature)

1 tsp mahlep (optional, see note below)

2 tsp baking powder

3 c flour

Topping:

Sesame seeds

2 egg whites

PREPARATION

Preheat oven to 375°F. Put the egg yolks, vinegar, corn oil, sugar and salt in a large bowl. Whisk them until the sugar and salt melt in the mixture. Whisk in the softened butter, mahlep, and baking powder. Slowly knead in the flour until you obtain a stiff non-sticky dough. (If you add the flour all at once, it will toughen the dough.) Grab walnut sized pieces of dough and shape them like a donut. Dip first into the egg whites and then sesame seeds, and place them onto a parchment paper lined baking pan. Bake the bagels for 20 minutes.

About Kandil Sesame Rings

These pastries are savory, ring-shaped biscuits baked and shared on holy days in Turkey. The biscuits themselves are not holy but remind people of the holy day which is observed by sharing them with neighbors and experiencing the spirituality of the day together. The sharing of Kandil sesame rings has become more popular since bakeries became more common.

About Mahlep

Mahlep is a spice obtained from Prunus mahaleb by cracking the cherry stones, extracting the seed kernel and grinding to a powder. Mahlep is used in small quantities to sharpen sweet foods, crisp savory cookies and also as a preservative. (Wikipedia)

TAHINI PASTRY (TAHINLI COREK)****

INGREDIENTS

Dough:

3⅓ c flour

3 tbsp plus 1 tsp sugar

2 tsp instant yeast

A pinch of salt

6 tbsp plus 2 tsp corn oil

1¼ c warm water

Tahini mixture:

⅔ lb tahini

1¼ c sugar

3 tbsp plus 1 tsp corn oil

Topping:

1 egg yolk

3 tbsp water

2 tbsp sugar

1 tsp sesame seeds

PREPARATION

Mix flour, sugar, yeast and the salt in a bowl. Put the oil and warm water in the center of the dry mixture and start kneading. When it reaches a soft consistency, sprinkle the top with flour and cover it with a moist towel. Let it rest for 45-60 minutes. While the dough is resting, prepare the tahini mixture by combining the ingredients listed above. After the dough has rested and risen, divide it into 8 pieces. Preheat the oven 350°F. Sprinkle some flour on a clean, dry counter top and use a rolling pin to flatten the pieces one by one. Make sure to flatten each piece as thin as it can be without tearing the dough. Carefully spread 2 to 3 tablespoons of the tahini mixture on each dough. Roll each up and stretch by holding at the ends and pulling as far as you can pull; don't worry about breaking the dough, if it breaks just press it back together. After stretching, roll it around itself in a spiral. Place it on a baking pan covered with parchment paper. Brush the tops with an egg wash made from 1 egg yolk and 3 tbsp of water and sprinkle with sugar and sesame seeds. Bake until browned, about 35 minutes.

TURKISH WATER PASTRY WITH CHEESE (KOLAY SU BOREGI)***

INGREDIENTS

4 eggs

1 c oil

2 c water

2 c milk

6 pieces Turkish phyllo dough

Filling

½ lb feta cheese

1 c finely chopped parsley

PREPARATION

Preheat oven to 375°F. Beat the eggs and mix with oil, water and milk. Spread one sheet of the dough onto a greased deep baking pan like a cake pan. The pan does not have to be the same size as the phyllo dough; you can cut and fold the phyllo to fit to the bottom of the pan. Roll up one piece of phyllo dough and cut into 3" slices. Dip the slices into the milk mixture, unroll, loosely layer and arrange the dough slices in the pan. Repeat with the rest of the phyllo dough pieces. Spread the feta cheese filling over the aranged dough slices. Roll and dip two more dough sheets and place on top of the feta filling. Lay the remaining dough sheets flat on top and sprinkle or brush with the remaining milk mixture. Bake for about 30 minutes and serve warm.

About Water Pastry

Water Pastry is named after with the use of water while being prepared. This pastry is particularly famous in Turkey for being hard to prepare and delicious to eat. Although it is a rather lengthy process to make this pastry, typically in Central and Northern Turkey there are several people preparing it together from scratch. It is also available in many bakeries.

This pastry is very famous by being light in taste, since all of the flattened dough pieces are boiled in water, cooled in cold water, drained, and finally baked. The following pastry is an easier version of the original, so that you can enjoy a similar taste with less effort.

ELITE DUMPLING (SOSYETE MANTISI)**

INGREDIENTS

Filling:

1 medium onion (chopped)

7 tbsp canola oil

⅔ lb ground beef

¼ tsp Salt

Pepper

Ground cumin

2 tbsp canola oil

⅔ c water

3 pieces Turkish phyllo dough

Dipping Sauce:

2 c plain yogurt

Garlic (to taste)

¼ c canola oil

2 tsp red pepper flakes

PREPARATION

Preheat the oven 400°F. Line a 9"x13" baking pan with parchment paper. Sauté onion in 7 tbsp oil and add ground beef and continue cooking for 5 minutes. Once the onion is translucent add salt, pepper and cumin. In a separate bowl, mix 2 tbsp canola oil with water. Place the circular sheets of phyllo dough on a flat surface and cut them into 4 quarters. Brush the dough with the water-oil mixture. Put 2 tablespoons of filling on the curved edge of each quarter of phyllo dough and roll up like a cigar. Then roll the dough in a spiral. Place each piece on baking dish and put ½ tablespoon of water-oil mixture on top of each roll. Bake until golden brown, about 20-25 minutes.

Heat ¼ c canola oil with red pepper flakes, cool. Mix chopped garlic with yogurt.. To serve dumpling garnish with yogurt and then the oil mix on top.

PUFFY BAGELS (ACMA)***

INGREDIENTS

2 c plus 1 tbsp flour

1 tsp salt

½ tsp sugar

1 tbsp instant yeast

⅔ c milk

½ c corn oil

2 tbsp butter

Topping:

1 egg yolk

Sesame seeds, poppy seeds or black cumin seeds

PREPARATION

Mix flour, salt, sugar and yeast in a deep bowl. Make a well in the middle and knead in milk and oil. Form a non-sticky dough and cover with a clean, damp cloth. Let it rise for about an hour until doubled in size. Take egg sized pieces of dough and roll out each piece to 4″-5″ in diameter. Gently spread each with about 1 tsp of butter. Roll up the dough, twist, and join the two ends. Repeat with remaining pieces of dough. Preheat oven to 400°F. Place the bagels about 2″ apart on a baking pan lined with parchment paper. Brush the tops with the egg yolk and sprinkle with sesame seeds, poppy seeds or black cumin seeds. Bake until golden brown, about 35 minutes.

DESSERTS

Delightful Turkish Desserts

- Cakes
- Cookies
- Dairy Desserts
- Custards
- Desserts with Syrup

MOLE DESSERT (KOSTEBEK PASTASI)****

INGREDIENTS

Cake:

3 eggs

1½ c sugar

1 tsp vanilla (or 1 packet vanilla sugar)

1 c milk

½ c oil

2½ c flour

1 tbsp baking powder

¼ c cocoa

Cream:

2 c milk

5 tbsp cornstarch

½ c + 2 tbsp sugar

5 tbsp cream cheese (room temperature)

½ c heavy whipping cream

1 tsp vanilla (or 1 packet vanilla sugar)

2 bananas (sliced)
Chocolate chips (optional)

PREPARATION

Preheat oven to 350°F and grease a 9"x13" baking dish. Mix eggs, sugar and vanilla with hand mixer. Add milk and oil and continue mixing. Next add flour, baking powder and cocoa, mix thoroughly. Bake 30-40 minutes until toothpick comes out clean.

Preparation of cream: *Mix milk, cornstarch and sugar thoroughly in a pot and cook over medium heat until thick. Let it cool. Stir in cream cheese, heavy whipping cream, and vanilla. Cut the cake into circles using a glass or biscuit cutter. Place one slice of banana, chocolate chips and 1 tbsp of cream on each. Make crumbles from remaining cake and sprinkle on the cakes to cover the cream.*

CARROT CAKE (HAVUCLU KEK)**

INGREDIENTS

4 large eggs

¾ c vegetable oil

2 c finely shredded carrots

2 c flour

2 c sugar

2 tsp baking powder

½ tsp baking soda

¾ tsp cinnamon

¾ c raisins

¾ c walnuts

PREPARATION

Preheat oven to 350°F and grease a 9"x13" baking pan. In a big bowl mix eggs, vegetable oil, and carrots. Combine flour, sugar, baking powder, baking soda, and cinnamon and add this to the carrot mixture. Beat at medium speed for about 5 minutes. Stir in the walnuts and the raisins. Bake 35-40 minutes.

TAHINI CAKE (TAHINLI KEK)**

INGREDIENTS

3 eggs

2 c sugar

1 c vegetable oil

1 c yogurt

2½ c flour

6 tbsp tahini (divided use)

1 tbsp baking powder

2 tsp sesame seeds

PREPARATION

Preheat the oven to 350°F. Beat eggs and sugar. Stir in all the rest of the ingredients except 3 tbsp of tahini. Spray a Bundt pan with oil and sprinkle with 1 tsp sesame seeds. Pour cake batter into the pan, drizzle with 3 tbsp of tahini and sprinkle with remaining sesame seeds. Bake for about an hour until an inserted toothpick comes out clean.

WET CAKE WITH FIGS (INCIRLI ISLAK KEK)****

INGREDIENTS

Cake:

3 eggs

1 c sugar

1 c walnut halves

1 c flour

1 tbsp baking powder

6 dried figs (soaked, drained and diced)

Pudding:

2 tbsp cornstarch

2 tbsp flour

4 c milk

5 tbsp sugar

3 tbsp butter

1 c heavy whipping cream

Syrup:

1½ cups water

1 tbsp instant coffee

½ cup sugar

PREPARATION

Preheat oven to 300°F. Beat eggs and sugar for 2 minutes. Mix in walnuts, flour and baking powder. Finally, add figs and pour the cake mixture into a 9″x13″ baking dish. Bake for 30 minutes. (The figs require the cake to be baked on low heat.)

In the meantime, prepare the pudding. Place all the pudding ingredients (except heavy whipping cream and butter) in a pan and cook over medium heat, stirring constantly. When it starts to boil add butter and cook one more minute. Turn the heat off and let the pudding cool. Whip the heavy whipping cream using a mixer. Stir whipped cream into the pudding and mix thoroughly. Let the cake cool for 3-4 minutes. Mix the syrup ingredients (do not cook) and pour onto the cake. 5 minutes later spread the pudding over the cake. Refrigerate 2-3 hours before serving.

CHOCOLATE CAKE ROLL (CIKOLATALI RULO PASTA)****

INGREDIENTS

Cake:

5 large eggs (divided use)

1 c powdered sugar

1 c flour

1 tsp vanilla (or 1 packet vanilla sugar)

1½ tsp baking powder

2 tbsp cocoa

Cream:

2 c milk

¾ c sugar

5 tbsp cornstarch (heaping)

3 tbsp cream cheese

½ c heavy whipping cream

1 tsp vanilla (or 1 packet vanilla sugar)

3 tbsp cocoa

Filling:

½ c chocolate chips

¼ c unsalted pistachios

Topping:

1/4 c chocolate chips

1 tbsp unsalted pistachios (ground)

3 tbsp chocolate syrup

PREPARATION

Preheat oven to 375°F and line a 10"x15" jelly roll pan with parchment paper. Separate 3 eggs, putting whites into one mixing bowl and yolks into another. Add the other 2 eggs into the bowl with the yolks and beat with a mixer. To this add powdered sugar and then flour, vanilla, baking powder, cocoa and mix thoroughly. Rinse beaters and beat the 3 egg whites with a pinch of salt until stiff peaks form. Then gently fold the egg whites into the cake batter; do not beat. Pour into prepared pan, gently spreading the cake batter out to an even thickness and bake for 7-10 minutes. Lay a piece of greased parchment paper on the counter and flip the hot cake out onto it. Remove and discard the parchment paper that had lined the pan. Turn the cake so that the long side is facing you. While still hot, gently roll the cake with the fresh parchment paper into a log. Let it cool seam side down.

Cook milk, sugar and cornstarch over medium heat until thick, stirring constantly. Stir pudding and let it cool. Then stir in cream cheese, heavy whipping cream, vanilla. Unroll the cake. Spread half of this cream over the surface of the cake, put chocolate chips and pistachios on one longer end and reroll the cake gently without the parchment paper. Spread the rest of the cream on top. Sprinkle coconut, chocolate chips, pistachios and chocolate syrup on top and serve.

BIRTHDAY CAKE WITH FRESH FRUITS (MEYVELI YAS PASTA)*****

INGREDIENTS

Cake:

5 eggs

1½ c powdered sugar

½ c flour

1 tsp vanilla (or 1 packet vanilla sugar)

1 tbsp baking powder

1 pinch salt

Pudding:

2 c milk

½ c + 2 tbsp sugar

5 tbsp cornstarch

5 tbsp cream cheese

½ c heavy whipping cream

1 tsp vanilla (or 1 packet vanilla sugar)

Filling:

5 strawberries (cut in ½" cubes)

1 banana (cut in ½" cubes)

1 kiwi (cut in ½" cubes)

For decoration:

Rolled fondant or more fruit

PREPARATION

Preheat oven to 375°F and lightly grease a deep 9-inch round spring-form pan. For cake, separate 3 eggs into whites and yolks in two bowls. Add the other 2 eggs into bowl with yolks and mix with an electric mixer. To this add powdered sugar, flour, vanilla and baking powder then mix thoroughly. In second bowl with 3 egg whites,(before beating egg whites,rinse beaters) add a pinch of salt and beat until stiff peaks form. Gently fold the egg whites into the cake batter; do not beat. Start baking the cake at 375°F until it has risen, then lower the temperature to 250°F. Bake for 20 minutes or longer until an inserted toothpick comes out clean. Cool on a rack before removing from the pan. Carefully cut the cake horizontally into three layers. It can be easier to cut even layers if the cake is on a turntable. (Alternatively you could bake the batter in three separate 9" pans, distributing the batter evenly so the layers are the same thickness.)

For cream, cook milk, sugar and cornstarch over medium heat until thick, stirring continuously. Cool. Then stir in cream cheese, heavy whipping cream, and vanilla, beating until smooth. Spread one third of the pudding over one cake layer and the bananas on top of it. Then put the second layer on top of it. Spread the half of the remaining pudding and the strawberries and kiwi over it. Finally place the third cake layer on the top and spread the remaining pudding all over the cake. To decorate, you can use rolled fondant and icing decorations or just fresh fruit.

COOKIES WITH MARMALADE (MARMELATLI KURABIYE)***

INGREDIENTS

1 c butter (diced and brought to room temperature)

1 c powdered sugar

1 tsp vanilla (or 1 packet vanilla sugar)

1 egg (separated)

2½ c flour

½ c sesame seeds

Filling:

½ c marmalade (or fruit preserves)

PREPARATION

Preheat the oven 375°F and grease a cookie sheet. In a bowl, mix butter, powdered sugar and vanilla with your hand. Mix in egg yolk and then flour and make a soft, non-sticky dough. Divide dough into two. Form into logs about 1-1½" in diameter. Roll the dough in egg white first and then in sesame seeds. Cut the dough into ½" slices. Place cookies on the cookie sheet and press in the middle of the cookies with your finger to create a well. Start baking, press gently onto the cookies with a ¼ teaspoon again halfway through and bake until cookies are golden brown. Cool the cookies and put ½ tsp marmalade or preserves in the middle of each.

APPLE COOKIES (ELMALI KURABIYE)***

INGREDIENTS

Filling:

3 medium apples (peeled and shredded)

3 tbsp sugar

1 tsp cinnamon

Dough:

1 c butter (room temperature)

¼ c water

½ c sugar

1 tbsp baking powder

1½ c flour

For top:

Powdered sugar

PREPARATION

Preheat oven 350°F. Mix all filling ingredients in a pot and cook them over medium heat until the juice from the apples evaporates. Let it cool. Put butter, water and sugar in a large bowl and knead well with your hands. Add flour and baking powder while kneading until you get non-sticky smooth soft dough. Make egg sized balls from the dough and flatten with the palms of your hands. Place 1 tsp of the filling and fold the two edges toward the center and seal in the middle. Continue with all dough pieces and place them on a baking sheet. Bake for 25 minutes. Cool, sprinkling with powdered sugar before serving.

CINNAMON AND TAHINI COOKIES (TARCINLI TAHINLI KURABIYE)***

INGREDIENTS

1 c butter (room temperature, diced)

½ c vegetable oil

5 tbsp tahini

½ tsp cinnamon

¼ c powdered sugar

1½ cup finely chopped walnuts or hazelnuts

Flour as needed

PREPARATION

Preheat the oven to 350°F and grease a cookie sheet or line it with parchment paper. Mix the butter, vegetable oil, tahini, cinnamon, powdered sugar and chopped nuts together. Add the flour until the dough is not sticking to your hand. Take hazelnut size balls from the dough and roll into balls. Bake the cookies for 10 to 15 minutes until golden brown.

WALNUT COOKIES (CEVIZLI KURABIYE)**

INGREDIENTS

¾ c butter

1 c powdered sugar

½ c walnuts (finely chopped)

1 tbsp baking powder

1 tsp vanilla (or 1 packet vanilla sugar)

1 egg yolk

2 c flour

1 egg white

25 walnut halves (for the tops)

PREPARATION

Preheat the oven to 350°F and line a cookie sheet with parchment paper. Mix all the ingredients except the flour, egg white, and walnuts. Add the flour slowly and make a soft dough. Make walnut-sized balls with your hands and place them on the cookie sheet. Whisk the egg white and brush the tops of the cookies. Place a walnut half on top of each and press in slightly. Bake for about 25-30 minutes until lightly browned.

TURKISH SHORTBREAD (UN KURABIYESI)**

INGREDIENTS

1 c butter (room temperature, diced)

5 tbsp vegetable oil

3 tbsp powdered sugar

¼ c cornstarch

3½ c flour

Topping:

½ c powdered sugar

PREPARATION

Preheat oven to 325° and line a cookie sheet with parchment paper. Beat butter, vegetable oil and powdered sugar until creamy. Add cornstarch and flour and knead gently to make a dough. Take about 1/10 of the dough roll into a 1" diameter log. Gently press along the log with a fork to make a decorative design. Cut the dough into 2" pieces. Repeat with the rest of the dough. Place on cookie sheet and bake for 15 minutes. The cookies should not brown. Let the cookies cool, and dust with powdered sugar before serving.

MUSHROOM CAP COOKIES (MANTAR KURABIYE)**

INGREDIENTS

2 c cornstarch

1½ c flour (divided use)

2 large eggs

1½ c powdered sugar

1 c butter

1 tsp vanilla (or 1 packet vanilla sugar)

1 tbsp baking powder

1 tbsp cocoa

PREPARATION

Preheat oven to 375°F and grease a cookie sheet. Make a soft non-sticky dough using all of the ingredients except cocoa. Make walnut sized balls and shape like a mushroom with the help of a water bottle lid: dip bottom of the lid into water and then cocoa and press gently onto the cookies. Bake for about 15 minutes, do not brown. Cool and serve.

MERINGUE (BEZE)***

INGREDIENTS

2 egg whites (room temperature)

1 c sugar

2-3 drops lemon juice

pinch of salt

PREPARATION

Preheat oven to 225-230°F. Line a cookie sheet with parchment paper. Beat egg whites with a mixer in a dry glass or steel bowl for about 5 minutes.. Then add ½ cup of sugar and whisk for 3 more minutes. Then add the rest of the sugar, lemon juice and salt and beat for an additional 15 minutes. You should get a cream-like consistency. Pipe or spoon meringues onto cookie sheet. Bake for 45 minutes. They should remain white once baked. At the end of the baking time, don't open the oven door. Turn off the heat and leave the meringues in the closed oven for at least 8 hours.

ORANGE & CHEESE-CURD COOKIES

INGREDIENTS

Filling:

Peel of 2 oranges (diced)

Water to cover (to boil orange peels)

½ c water

½ c sugar

5.3 oz cheese curds (See "Extras" chapter)

Dough:

5 c flour (add ½ c flour as needed)

½ c sugar

1 tbsp baking powder

1 c plus 2 tbsp butter (cubed)

½ c olive oil

½ c yogurt

1 tsp vanilla

½ c powdered sugar

PREPARATION

Place orange peels in water to cover and bring to a boil. Drain and change water and bring to a second boil. Repeat the process once more to remove the bitterness of the peels. Finally add the water and sugar and bring to a boil for the fourth time. Allow to boil until the water evaporates. Cool and mix with cheese curds.

Preheat oven to 350°F. Put flour in a big bowl and mix in the sugar and baking powder. Make a well in the middle for the cubed butter. Add olive oil, yogurt, and vanilla on top of the butter. Mix wet ingredients with your hand. Start kneading the dough by slowly mixing in the dry ingredients from the sides to the middle of the bowl. Form a soft smooth dough. Take golf ball sized pieces, flatten and place 1 tsp filling in the middle of each and draw up edges into a bundle and pinch to seal. Place on a baking pan with seam side down. Bake cookies until lightly browned, about 25 minutes. Sprinkle with powdered sugar and serve.

SEMOLINA HALVAH WITH ICE CREAM (DONDURMALI IRMIK HELVASI)***

INGREDIENTS

2 c milk

2 c water

3 c sugar (divided use)

1 c butter

½ c pine nuts

2 c semolina

Filling/ Topping:

Ice cream

PREPARATION

Boil milk and water with 1½ cups sugar to make a syrup. In a separate pot, stir pine nuts with butter over low heat, add semolina and fry until nuts turn golden. Turn off the heat, pour the syrup on the semolina mixture and blend well. Keep on the stove and cover, letting it sit until all of the syrup is absorbed. Remove the pot from the stove and add the rest of the sugar, mix very well and cover. After 5 min stir halvah again, cover and cool for 15 minutes. Serve with ice cream either on top or in the middle as pictured.

Halvah: *Halvah is a very famous dessert in Turkey and several Middle Eastern countries. In Turkey two main types of halvah are flour halvah and semolina halvah. Halvah is made when a child is born, when somebody passes away, when somebody is called for military service, or when somebody returns from the pilgrimage to Mecca. When halvah is made, it is made in large quantities and shared with neighbors and relatives.*

Maras Ice Cream: *It has been made since the 18th century. It is distinguished from all other ice creams because of a special ingredient and the preparing technique. This special ingredient is called "sahlep" which is obtained from the knobby root of a wild orchid, "Dactylorhiza osmanica", and ground in a mill. The preparation technique specific for this ice cream is about how it is treated after it reached common ice-cream consistency. The ice cream is then pounded with metal or wooden rod with a flat end like a paddle for about 20 minutes to develop its elasticity. It reaches a stiff consistency that it can even be hung on a hook. This is the part that makes Maras Ice Cream to have a smooth texture yet hard enough to be cut with knives for serving. You can have it in cups, cones or waffle sandwiches.*

GULLAC***

INGREDIENTS

7 c milk

2 c sugar

1 tbsp rose water (optional)

10 gullac sheets

Topping:

⅓ c unsalted pistachios (chopped)

1 c Pomegranate seeds

⅓ c hazelnut (chopped)

⅓ c walnut (chopped)

PREPARATION

Put milk, sugar and rosewater in a pot and heat over low heat until the sugar melts, stirring occasionally. Remove from the stove and let it sit for about 20 minutes. Lay a gullac sheet on a 10"x 15" jelly roll pan (1" deep). Wet it with the lukewarm milk mixture. Repeat this with ten sheets, stacking one on top of the other. When you finish with the tenth one, pour the rest of the milk mixture over. They do not need to be perfectly arranged. They will combine when they get wet with milk. After pouring the milk, you will see the sheets are rising, do not touch them. Cover with stretch film and refrigerate for at least 2 hours. After taking it from refrigerator, cut it in squares or rectangles. When you are ready to serve, garnish with 1 tsp nuts and 1 tbsp pomegranate seeds per serving.

Gullac Sheets: *Gullac is a Turkish dessert made with milk, pomegranate and gullac sheets. It is consumed especially during Ramadan in Turkey. Gullac sheets are basically starch wafers that are made of cornstarch, flour and water. The word gullac comes from "Gullu As" which means "Food with roses." Although the dessert itself may contain rose petals and rose syrup, the name actually refers to the shape of layers which look similar to rose petals. Gullac sheets are very hard to make at home, since they require special equipment including pans to dry the sheets. Mediterranean stores, international food markets, and Turkish stores might carry packages of gullac sheets. Please refer to the introduction chapter for contact information for some of these vendors.*

KATAIFI WITH PUDDING (MUHALLEBILI KADAYIF)**

INGREDIENTS

5 c kataifi (shredded phyllo dough) (chopped)

5 tbsp butter.

Pudding:

3 tbsp cornstarch

1 tbsp flour

6 c milk

5 tbsp sugar

1 tsp vanilla (or 1 packet vanilla sugar)

2 tbsp cream cheese

PREPARATION

Cook kataifis with butter in a pan over medium heat until golden brown, stirring constantly. In a deep pot, mix cornstarch, flour, milk and sugar and cook over medium heat until it becomes thick, stirring constantly. Let it cool and stir occasionally. Stir in vanilla and cream cheese and beat for 3-4 minutes until smooth. Spread the kataifi in a 9"x13" baking pan to cover the whole surface. Pour the pudding over to cover the kataifi. Refrigerate for 4-5 hrs. Cut into 4"x6" slices and roll up each slice to have the kataifi side outside and pudding inside. Place on the serving plate with seam side down.

Kataifi: *Kataifi is a form of phyllo dough made with wheat and water. However, this dough is shredded. Traditionally kataifi is used to make the famous Kataifi dessert, but it could also be used in savory dishes. You can form kataifi into cones, shells or nests, or you can layer them. Many Middle Eastern grocery stores stock kataifi.*

TIRAMISU**

INGREDIENTS

1 c sugar

2 c milk

1 egg yolk

2 tbsp flour

8 oz package cream cheese

24 ladyfinger cookies

2 tbsp instant coffee

1 tbsp sugar

2 c water

Cocoa powder (unsweetened, for garnish)

PREPARATION

Combine sugar, milk, egg yolk and flour and cook over medium heat, stirring constantly, until it becomes pudding. Blend in the cream cheese with a mixer. Place the lady fingers side by side on a 9'x13" baking pan. Mix instant coffee, sugar and water. Spoon half of the coffee mixture over the ladyfingers and then half of the pudding over that. Make a second layer with the rest of the lady fingers and spread the coffee mixture. Finally, spread the remaining pudding all over. Cover and refrigerate overnight. Sprinkle with cocoa powder before serving.

Note: *This is best made a day in advance.*

WHITE MOSAIC TEA BISCUIT DESSERT**

INGREDIENTS

3-6 oz packages tea biscuits (18 oz total)

14 oz dried figs (diced)

2 bananas (diced)

2 kiwis (diced)

1 c crushed walnuts

2 c heavy whipping cream

2 c powdered sugar

Topping:

Chocolate syrup

PREPARATION

Crush tea biscuits. In a deep bowl, beat heavy whipping cream with powdered sugar until stiff peaks form. Mix in crushed tea biscuits, fruit and crushed walnuts. Line a pan with plastic wrap. Pour the mixture into the lined pan. Using the plastic wrap, shape the mixture into a pyramid and freeze for 1 hour. Remove the plastic wrap, slice, garnish with chocolate syrup and serve.

Tea biscuits: *Turkish Tea biscuits (for example "Ulker" brand) can be found online (Amazon) or you may substitute "Kedem Tea Biscuits" or "Le Petit Beurre" brands. One 6 oz package has 25 tea biscuits. They taste similar to animal crackers.*

Whipping Cream: *You may find whipping cream in three different versions: powdered whipping cream, heavy whipping cream, and non-dairy whipped topping like Cool Whip. Turkish recipes usually call for powdered whipping cream mix. The powdered whipping cream is mixed with milk and beaten with a mixer until stiff peaks form. For your convenience we have substituted powdered whipping cream with heavy whipping cream.*

AFRICAN DREAM (AFRIKA RUYASI)**

INGREDIENTS

2 c heavy whipping cream

2 c powdered sugar

4 c tea biscuits (crushed)

2 tbsp instant coffee

¼ tsp vanilla

1½ c walnuts (crushed)

¼ c chocolate chips

1 banana (diced)

Topping:

Chocolate sauce

Ground pistachio, shredded coconut and chopped walnut (optional garnish)

PREPARATION

In a deep bowl, beat heavy whipping cream with powdered sugar until stiff peaks form. Crush tea biscuits. Stir in instant coffee, vanilla, walnuts, crushed tea biscuits, chocolate chips and banana. Line 9" bundt cake mold with plastic wrap pour the dessert in. Refrigerate for 3-4 hours. Flip the pan on a plate, remove plastic wrap and decorate with chocolate sauce. Optionally you may add pistachio, coconut and walnut.

TRUFFS*

INGREDIENTS

½ c butter

1 tbsp sugar

3 tbsp cocoa

1 c milk

1-6 oz package tea biscuit (25 pieces)

½ c walnuts (chopped)

Topping options:

Oatmeal, coconuts, grated chocolate

PREPARATION

Melt the butter in a saucepan. Mix in sugar and cocoa. Stir in 1 cup of milk and cook on medium heat for 5 minutes, stirring constantly. In another bowl crush tea biscuits into small pieces. Pour the milk mixture on the biscuits. Stir in walnuts. Once cool enough to touch, knead for 2-3 minutes. Make walnut sized balls and roll in oatmeal, coconuts or grated chocolate.

CREAM-CAKE WITH BISCUITS (BISKUVILI PASTA)***

INGREDIENTS

2 c milk

¾ c sugar

¼ c cornstarch

3 tbsp cream cheese or labneh cheese

½ c heavy whipping cream or milk

2 tsp vanilla

2-6 oz packages petit beurre tea biscuits

To soak the biscuits:

1 c milk

Topping:

Chocolate sauce

PREPARATION

Mix milk, sugar and cornstarch in a pan. Cook it while stirring, until it has a pudding-like consistency. After preparing the pudding, stir it once in a while until it cools. Then pour in cream cheese (or labneh cheese), heavy whipping cream (or milk) and vanilla and beat with a mixer for 10 minutes until smooth.

Place one layer of biscuits on a 9"x13" pan in two rows (No need to cover the bottom of the pan. The dessert is easier to decorate with only two rows in the pan). Pour 1 tsp of milk over each biscuit and then spread the cream mixture on top. Repeat this process until you've used all of the biscuits (to obtain a stack of 7-8 layers). Decorate with chocolate sauce. Optionally you may put banana, chocolate and walnut between the layers.

CUSTARDS

CUSTARD WITH CHOCOLATE SAUCE (CIKOLATA SOSLU MUHALLEBI)***

INGREDIENTS

Custard:

4 c milk

1 c flour

1 c sugar

½ c butter

Chocolate sauce:

½ c butter

3 tbsp unsweetened cocoa powder

2 tbsp powdered sugar

2 egg yolks

PREPARATION

Mix all of the custard ingredients except butter and cook on medium-low heat until it boils. Turn the heat off and add the butter. Whip the custard with a mixer for 10 minutes. Pour into small glass bowls or serving dishes and let them cool. Melt the butter for the chocolate sauce, add powdered sugar and cocoa and whisk until smooth. Then stir in egg yolks one by one and beat with a mixer. Pour the sauce over the custard. Refrigerate at least two hours and serve.

ALMOND PUDDING (KESKUL)*

INGREDIENTS

egg yolks

¾ c sugar

4 c milk

2 tbsp cornstarch (melted with 3 tbsp water in a small cup)

½ c almond powder (or chopped almonds)

Ground unsalted pistachios, shredded coconut (to garnish)

PREPARATION

Beat the egg yolks, then whisk in sugar, cornstarch and milk. Cook over medium heat, stirring constantly. Add the almonds when you see the bubbles on the surface. Boil for one more minute while stirring. Take it off the stove. Pour into small serving bowls. Let them cool for an hour. Sprinkle with some ground pistachio and/or shredded coconut. Cover with plastic wrap and chill at least one hour before serving.

NOAH'S PUDDING (ASURE)*****

PREPARATION

INGREDIENTS

1 c shelled wheat (boiled until tender and drained)

1 c canned chickpeas (drained and rinsed)

1 c canned cannellini beans (drained and rinsed) (optional)

2 tbsp rice

½ c golden raisins

½ c dried apricots (diced)

½ c dried figs (diced)

2 tbsp rose water

6 whole cloves (½c water (for cloves))

5 c hot water

3 c sugar

Pinch of salt

Walnuts, hazelnuts (chopped, optional for garnish)

Cinnamon, currants and pomegranate (optional for garnish)

Place shelled wheat in a pot and add water to cover. Bring to a boil and simmer for 30 minutes. Drain the wheat and add back to the pot with fresh, hot water. Return to a boil. Turn the heat off and set aside for 2 hours. Drain. Boil rice in a small pot in water to cover for 10 minutes. Drain. Boil raisins, apricots and figs in three separate saucepans with enough water to cover the fruit for about 5 minutes. Drain.

Boil cloves in ½ cup of water for 5 minutes and reserve the liquid, discarding the cloves.

Combine wheat, chickpeas, cannellini beans, rice, raisins, apricots and figs in a big pot. Add 5 cups of hot water, the water from the cloves and rose water. Bring to a boil and continue to boil over medium- low heat for 20 minutes. Mix in the sugar and a pinch of salt. Continue to boil for 15-20 minutes. Turn the heat off. Pour into a serving bowl while still warm. Serve cool. Garnish with nuts and pomegranate seeds if you'd like.

Story of Noah's Pudding

5000 years ago God decided to destroy the world because of mankind's sin. One righteous man named Noah, however, found favor with God. Prophet Noah called his people to the religion of God for hundreds of years. When people rejected his ideas, continuing their wicked ways, God instructed Noah to build an ark. When the ark was built, Noah and his believers got on it with a two of all living creatures, both male and female. Then the punishment from God arrived in the form of a flood, such that no one could be saved other than those on the ark. When Noah's ark landed on Mount Ararat (in eastern Turkey) after the flood, Noah and his friends prepared a special dish to celebrate landing. This special dish contained a little bit of everything left in the ark: grains, dried fruits, figs, nuts, wheat, chickpeas, almonds and apricots. It turned out to be a delicious, sweet, rich dish called "Ashure" passing from generation to generation to be cooked and shared with family, friends and neighbors. Sharing Noah's Pudding is a sign of peace and understanding.

RICE PUDDING (SUTLAC)**

INGREDIENTS

½ c white medium-grain rice (washed and drained)

1½ c water

4 c milk (divided use)

1 c sugar

A pinch of salt

2 tbsp cornstarch

PREPARATION

Boil rice in 1½ cups of water until softened. In a separate bowl mix cornstarch with 1 cup milk. Bring the other 3 cups of milk to a boil, mix in the rice with water. Temper starch mix with 3-4 tbsp of boiling milk and slowly add into the pan while stirring. Add sugar and a pinch of salt and boil for 10 more minutes while stirring. Pour into heat resistant bowls. Pour some water in a 9"x13" cake pan and place bowls with rice pudding in it. Brown tops of the pudding under the broiler, cool, and remove from water bath. Refrigerate before serving.

TAHINI PUDDING (TAHINLI MUHALLEBI)***

INGREDIENTS

Pudding:

4 c milk

3 tbsp rice flour

3 tbsp cornstarch (or wheat starch)

1 c sugar

Tahini mixture:

1 c tahini

1 c milk

¼ c powdered sugar

Topping:

Sesame seeds (to your taste)

PREPARATION

Preheat oven to 350°F. Mix the pudding ingredients in a pan and bring to a boil over medium heat, stirring constantly until creamy. Pour into heat resistant serving bowls and cool for 5 minutes. Blend the ingredients for the tahini mixture in a separate bowl. Pour on top of the pudding bowls and sprinkle with sesame seeds. Bake for about 20 minutes being careful not to overcook the tahini. Cool 15 minutes and refrigerate at least one hour before serving.

COCOA SEMOLINA PUDDING (KAKAOLU IRMIK TATLISI)*

INGREDIENTS

4 c milk

¾ c sugar

½ c semolina

3 tbsp of cocoa

2 tbsp butter

Topping:

Pistachios

PREPARATION

Cook milk, sugar and semolina over medium heat, stirring constantly, boiling for 5 minutes. Continue cooking as needed until it reaches a pudding-like consistency. Off the heat, add cocoa and butter and mix it until the cocoa completely dissolves. Cool. Cover with a plastic wrap before putting in refrigerator. Serve cold with pistachios or other nuts you like.

CUSTARD WITH MASTIC GUM (SAKIZLI MUHALLEBI)**

INGREDIENTS

1 c sugar

1 tbsp cornstarch

4 tbsp flour

1/8 tsp mastic gum

5 c milk

1½ tsp butter

1 tsp vanilla

Topping:

½ c shredded coconut

Banana, kiwi, strawberry and blackberry (optional)

PREPARATION

Put the sugar, cornstarch, flour and mastic gum into a heavy saucepan, and blend in the milk. Bring the mixture to a boil over medium heat, stirring until a pudding-like consistency. Off the stove, add butter and vanilla and beat 5-6 minutes until smooth. Pour into individual serving dishes or one large dish and refrigerate 4-5 hours before serving. Top with shredded coconut and optional fruits.

MASTIC GUM:

Mastic is obtained from mastic trees found in 'Sakiz'(Gum) island and in Aegean region of Turkey. It is very rarely found and produced in small amount. Commonly used in making cookies and dairy desserts to enrich the flavor. You may substitute mastic gum with mastic gum flavored gums such as 'Falim' brand which is available online.

WATER PUDDING (SU MUHALLEBISI)*

INGREDIENTS

3 c water

2 c milk

⅔ c sugar

1 tbsp rose water

⅔ c cornstarch

Topping:

Powdered sugar

Banana, kiwi, strawberry (optional)

PREPARATION

Mix water, milk, sugar, rose water and cornstarch in a deep pot. Cook the mixture over medium heat, stirring continuously until it gets a pudding-like consistency. Pour into single-serve bowls. Refrigerate for at least 2-3 hours. When serving, invert the bowls onto dessert plates. Sprinkle with powdered sugar and decorate with fresh fruits as desired.

RIDDLED COOKIES (KALBURABASTI)****

INGREDIENTS

Syrup:

2½ c water

2½ c sugar

Juice of ¼ lemon

Dough:

1 c butter (at room temperature)

3 c flour

2 tbsp yogurt

2 tbsp vegetable oil

1 egg

1 tbsp baking powder

Filling:

1 cup crushed walnuts

PREPARATION

Boil water with sugar. After 10-15 minutes, add lemon juice. Boil for a minute and remove from the heat to cool to room temperature. For the dough, mix butter and flour with your hand. Add yogurt, oil, egg and baking powder. Knead until the dough is soft. Cover it with a wet towel and let it rest for 10 minutes. Preheat oven to 375°F. Divide the dough into walnut sized balls. Flatten and place 4-5 pieces walnut in the middle of each. Bring the sides together to enclose the nuts. To obtain a riddled look, gently press each the bottom of each dough ball against the holes of a grater or colander. Place the dough, seam side down, on a jelly roll pan. Bake for 10-15 minutes. Remove from the oven and pour syrup over the hot cookies.

BUTTERNUT SQUASH DESSERT (KABAK TATLISI)***

INGREDIENTS

1 large butternut squash (3 lbs)

3 c sugar

1 c chopped walnuts

PREPARATION

Cut squash in half and scoop out seeds and pulp. Peel and cut into 1" chunks. Place them in a pot and add sugar. Cover and simmer over medium-low heat for 40 minutes or until tender. To keep the pieces of squash intact, resist the temptation to stir the squash while it is cooking. Remove from heat, uncover and allow to cool. Cover and refrigerate for two hours. Garnish each serving with 2 tsp walnut.

FLAT KATAIFI (YASSI KADAYIF)*****

PREPARATION

INGREDIENTS

Syrup:

1 c sugar

1 c water

4-5 drops lemon juice

Batter:

1 c water

1 c milk

1½ c flour

1 tsp yeast

1 tsp sugar

¼ tsp salt

Filling:

1 cup walnuts (chopped)

To dip:

1 egg

Frying:

4 c oil (corn or vegetable oil)

Boil sugar with water. When it starts to boil, add lemon juice and let it boil 5 more minutes. Turn off the heat, let it cool.

Mix all batter ingredients in a deep bowl. Put aside, let it stand for 30 min. Pour 2 tbsp of batter onto a hot, dry non-stick pan. If you have one, use a silicone egg ring with a diameter of 4" so your kataifis are of a uniform size. Fry only one side and remove with the help of a spatula. Place to a plate and continue the process with the rest of the batter. On each kataifi place 1-2 tsp chopped walnuts. Fold pancake in half so the uncooked side is inside and the fried side is outside. Pinch the edges to tightly close each kataifi and safely enclose the walnuts. Whisk the egg and dip only the seam edges. Heat oil in a deep frying pan. Fry kataifis in oil for 2 minutes per side until lightly browned, put the kataifis into the syrup. Let them soak for 1-2 minutes and remove from the syrup. Garnish with some chopped walnuts and serve.

LOKMA DESSERT

There is a very famous Turkish dessert similar to Flat Kataifi called Lokma dessert. Lokma means "a morsel" which is a bite-size crunchy fried sweet dough that is covered in syrup. Lokma is served as a dessert with coffee. Lokma dough is made with flour, vegetable oil, yeast, sugar and salt. This mixture is poured into hot oil in different shapes as small balls, as a rod with straight lines on it or as a circle. In some regions of Turkey lokma is fried in oil but instead of being covered in syrup is served as a bread with cheese. The round version of Lokma dessert is called "The Palace Lokma." You may find Lokma sellers in Turkey on some special religious days.

CYPRUS DESSERT (KIBRIS TATLISI)****

INGREDIENTS

Syrup:

2½ c sugar

2 c water

Dough:

1 c sugar

4 eggs

1 c breadcrumbs

1 c coconut

1 c vegetable oil

1 tbsp baking powder

1 tsp vanilla

Cream:

1 c sugar

1 c coconut

1 c cornstarch

4 c milk

PREPARATION

Preheat oven to 375° F. Boil sugar and water for syrup and let it cool. Mix sugar and eggs until spongy. Blend in the other ingredients and pour the mixture into an oiled 9″x13″ glass baking dish. Bake for about 30 minutes. Pour cooled syrup over the hot desert and let it soak. For cream, mix the dry ingredients, add the milk, and cook until thickened. Cool 5-10 minutes and spread onto dessert.

SHEKERPARE (SEKERPARE)****

PREPARATION

Preheat oven to 500°F. Mix dough ingredients, adding flour carefully to make soft dough. Roll walnut-sized balls of dough and flatten a little bit. Place on a jellyroll pan and put one hazelnut on top of each. Place pan to the oven and reduce the heat to 350°F. While shekerpares are baking, make the syrup. Mix sugar, water and lemon juice in a pot and boil for 3-4 minutes. Remove from the heat. Take shekerpares out of the oven before they get brown and pour syrup on them.

INGREDIENTS

Dough:

1 c powdered sugar

1 c butter

2 eggs

½ c semolina

1 tbsp baking powder

3 c flour

Syrup:

6 c sugar

6 c water

1 tbsp lemon juice

SEMOLINA DESSERT (SAMBALI)***

INGREDIENTS

2 c semolina

1 c sugar

1 c yogurt

2 tsp vanilla (or 2 packets vanilla sugar)

2 tsp baking powder

½ c blanched almonds

Syrup:

3 c sugar

2 c water

1 tsp lemon juice

PREPARATION

Preheat oven to 350°F and grease a 10"x15" jellyroll pan. Mix semolina, sugar, yogurt, and vanilla in a large bowl. Beat the mixture, add baking powder and beat for 2 more minutes. Pour the mixture into prepared pan and spread evenly. Top with almonds. Bake it approximately 35-40 minutes until golden brown.

While sambali is baking, prepare the syrup. Boil sugar, water and lemon juice for 5 minutes. Take the sambali from the oven and pour the syrup over it. Both the cake and the syrup will be hot. After the cake absorbs the syrup, let it cool in the refrigerator. Serve the dessert at room temperature. Tip: Sambali tastes better if you prepare it the day before you serve it.

TOASTED BREAD DESSERT (ETIMEK TATLISI)***

INGREDIENTS

10-12 plain, unsalted Melba toasts (4 oz)

2 c sugar

2 c boiling water

3 c milk

3 tbsp flour

2 tsp vanilla

1 c whipping cream

2 tbsp sugar

Garnish:

Any kind of nuts or coconut

PREPARATION

Place the Melba toasts in a 9"x13" glass baking dish. Melt sugar over medium heat, stirring constantly. Cook 2-3 minutes longer until it is like caramel. Then carefully add the 2 cups of boiling water (stay away from the steam, hold the lid to protect yourself). Stir and boil the syrup for a couple of minutes. Pour the syrup on toasted breads and cool. In a pot, mix milk, flour and vanilla. Cook over medium heat, stirring constantly until thick like a pudding. Pour over the toasts topped with syrup. Cool completely. Whip cream with sugar. Spread this cream on the pudding as the third and last layer. Refrigerate at least one hour, garnish with nuts or coconut, and serve.

ROLLED BAKLAVA****

PREPARATION

INGREDIENTS

1-16 oz package Athens brand phyllo dough (Size #4)

1 c butter, melted

3 cups finely chopped walnuts

Syrup:

2½ c sugar

2½ c water

Few drops of lemon juice

If your phyllo dough is frozen, defrost in the refrigerator. Bring the phyllo to room temperature before beginning. Lay out two layers of phyllo dough and sprinkle with 1 tablespoon of melted butter. Spread 2 tablespoons of walnuts on phyllo and roll up, around a thin stick or rod if you have one. Slowly squeeze the roll from the sides to the center to give a gathered look. If you used one, remove the stick carefully. Cut the roll into 4 equal pieces, place onto a baking pan, keeping the rolls next to each other to prevent unrolling. Preheat oven to 350°F. Repeat with other layers of phyllo dough. Spoon remaining melted butter on top and bake until golden brown.

In a separate pot boil sugar and water. Add lemon juice and boil for 5 more minutes. Remove from heat to cool a bit. Pour warm syrup onto cooled baklava.

BAKLAVA

The creator of baklava is not known, but it has been an important dessert in Turkish kitchens for a long time. The current form of baklava was shaped during the Ottoman empire in Istanbul.

There is research suggesting that baklava made with layered breads were created by Turks in Central Asia. The Azerbaijani dish "Baku pakhlavasi" was made with nuts but not with the thin phyllo dough. Apparently, several nations contributed to the baklava we know today.

In the Ottoman military Janissary corps, soldiers were served trays of baklava on 15th of Ramadan in a ceremonial procession called the Baklava Alayı. (Modified from Binnur's Cookbook)

BAKLAVA****

INGREDIENTS

2-16 oz packages Athens brand phyllo dough (Size #4)

2 c pistachio (finely chopped)

1 c butter

Syrup:

4 c sugar

3 c water

½ c lemon juice

PREPARATION

Preheat the oven 375°F and grease a 9"x13" baking dish. Prepare syrup: boil sugar with water. When it starts to boil add lemon juice and let it boil for 5 more minutes. Turn off the heat, let it cool. Place 1½ packages phyllo in pan, sprinkle with chopped pistachios. Place rest of the phyllo on the top and cut into square or diamond shapes. Pour melted butter on slowly, and bake until light brown, about 25-30 minutes. Remove from the oven and pour hot syrup over the hot baklava.

PEAR WITH CUSTARD (KREMALI ARMUT TATLISI)****

INGREDIENTS

3 large pears (Korean pears, 12 oz total)

1½ c sugar

3-4 drops red food coloring

5 whole cloves

2 c water

For cream:

1 c milk

6 tbsp sugar

2 tbsp cornstarch

2 tbsp cream cheese (optional labneh)

½ c heavy whipping cream

1 tbsp vanilla

Topping:

Fresh mint leaves

PREPARATION

Peel pears and cut in half lengthwise. Remove the seeds and put the pears in a large pot. Add sugar, food coloring, and cloves. Add water until the pears are covered and boil until they soften. Stir gently while cooking, turning the pears occasionally. Remove the pears and place cut side up on the serving dish. Meanwhile, prepare the cream: mix milk, sugar and cornstarch in a pot and cook until it has a pudding-like consistency. Cool, then add cream cheese, heavy whipping cream and vanilla and beat for 10 minutes until smooth. Spoon or pipe cream into the hollows left by the pear's pit and decorate with fresh mint leaves.

SHOBIYET*****

INGREDIENTS

1-16 oz package Athens brand phyllo dough (Size #4)

1 c butter

Syrup:

3 c sugar

2 c water

Juice of half of a lemon

Cream:

¾ c + 1 tbsp semolina

5 c milk

Filling:

1 c pistachios (chopped)

Topping:

1 c pistachios (chopped)

PREPARATION

Preheat oven to 350°F. Prepare syrup: Boil sugar with water. When it starts to boil add lemon juice and let it boil for 5 more minutes. Set aside to cool. In another pot, mix semolina with milk over medium heat, and stir until thick. Set aside to cool. Take 7 pieces of phyllo dough and cut widthwise into 4 pieces. Then cut in half lengthwise to obtain 8 squares. On each 7-layer square put 1 tsp cream and 1 tsp chopped pistachios. Fold them on the diagonal and place the triangles on a jelly roll pan. Place the second piece on the seam side of the first to keep it closed. Repeat with other pieces of phyllo dough. Melt the butter in a pan and pour over the sobiyet. Bake until light brown, about 20 minutes. Remove from the oven and pour warm syrup over the hot shobiyet. Sprinkle with chopped pistachios and serve.

ROSE DESSERT (GUL TATLISI)****

INGREDIENTS

For syrup:

2 c water

2 c sugar

¼ tsp lemon juice

Dough:

2 eggs

¼ c powdered sugar

1½ c butter

1 package vanillin sugar

1 tbsp baking powder

1 tsp apple cider vinegar

¼ tsp salt

2 c flour

To decorate:

Hazelnut

Pistachio (optional)

PREPARATION

Preheat oven to 375°F. First prepare syrup. Boil sugar with water. When it starts to boil add lemon juice and let it boil for 5 more minutes. Turn off the heat, let it cool. Mix all of the dough ingredients except flour in a bowl. Add flour slowly and knead the dough thoroughly. Divide the dough into three equal pieces. Roll out each piece to ½″ thickness and cut out circles with a 2″ cookie or biscuit cutter. Lay four of the circles in a row, overlapping their ends so together they are about 4″ in length. Roll up the circles, press and seam the edges tighten the roll. You will obtain a 2.5″ x 2.5″ cylindrical dough. Cut the roll in the middle and place the pieces on baking dish cut side down; each small roll will make two "roses." Place a hazelnut in the middle of each "rose." Shape all dough in the same way. Bake about 25-30 minutes until golden brown. Remove from the oven and pour cool syrup on it. Dessert is ready to serve after one hour.

EXTRAS

Breakfast in Turkey

In Turkish, breakfast is called "kahvaltı", derived from "kahve altı", which literally means "before coffee". As the name implies, traditionally Turkish coffee is not served during breakfast, rather after breakfast or in the afternoon. Traditionally brewed black tea is a must for Turkish breakfast. Along with hot black tea, white cheese (feta cheese), boiled or scrambled eggs, green or black olives, cokelek (spicy cheese), Turkish sausage, halva, pekmez (grape or mulberry molasses), tomatoes, cucumbers, honey, jam, fresh butter, an omelet called "menemen", fresh warm bread and Simit (sesame bagel) complete the Turkish breakfast. Occasionally, fried potatoes and various types of pastries are also served along.

Breakfast in Turkey is not only about food, but also about family time and gathering. During especially the weekends, people invite their friends or relatives over for breakfast. Tea will be served all the time not to interrupt people having quality conversations during the breakfast.

Turkish Black Tea, Teapot and Tea Glass

When Turkish people wake up in the morning, the first thing they do is boil water for Turkish Tea. Black tea is harvested in the eastern Black Sea region of Turkey. It is brewed using two stacked kettles specifically designed for this purpose. Turkey is one of the largest tea markets in the world. In the last decade, Turkey had the highest per capita tea consumption in the world.

TURKISH BLACK TEA (CAY)*

INGREDIENTS

2 tbsp black tea

6 c water (divided use)

PREPARATION

Commonly-used Turkish teapots have two parts: an upper part for tea leaves and a bottom part for boiling water. Put black tea leaves into the upper part, add 4 cups of water into the bottom part, set the upper part on the bottom part, and bring to a boil. Lower the heat, simmer for 3-4 minutes, and then pour 2½ cups of it onto the tea leaves. Then add 2 cups of cold water to the bottom of the teapot. Bring it to a second boil and lower the heat. When the tea leaves sink, your tea is ready. To serve, fill a tea glass less than half full of tea. Then add an equal amount of hot water from the bottom part of your teapot, leaving some space so the glass is not too hot to hold. Optionally you may add ½ tsp of sugar per glass. Serve immediately as it tastes best hot and because the tea leaves in your teapot can turn bitter the longer they sit.

TURKISH COFFEE (TURK KAHVESI)**

INGREDIENTS

2 heaping tsp Turkish coffee

1 tsp sugar

1½ c water

PREPARATION

To make authentic Turkish coffee you will need a cezve coffee pot (as shown in the picture). In this pot add water, coffee and sugar. Stir briefly over low-medium heat and let it come to a boil very slowly. Just before it boils spoon the foam on top into your serving cups. Bring it to a boil and pour the coffee on top of the foam slowly so as not to disturb it. The foamier your coffee, the better. Serve with some Turkish delight, a piece of chocolate or baklava.

About Turkish coffee: *Turkish coffee is prepared using a narrow-topped small pot called a cezve. Traditionally, the pot is made of copper and has a wooden handle. The ingredients are finely ground coffee, cold water and (if desired) sugar. It is served in a fincan with Turkish delight or chocolate. The same teaspoon is used both for measuring the coffee and sugar and for stirring. A moderately low heat is used so that the coffee does not come to the boil too quickly—the ground coffee needs to be in hot water for long enough to extract the flavor. As with any other sort of coffee, the best Turkish coffee is made from freshly roasted beans ground just before brewing. Turkish style grounded beans can be bought and stored as any other type, although it loses flavor with time.*

Turkish delight: *Turkish delight (lokum) is a gel-based dessert made with starch and sugar. Variations are made with rosewater, mastic or fruit flavors. Chopped hazelnuts, pistachios, or walnuts may also be added. Lokum is often packaged in small cubes dusted with powdered sugar. You will find that frequently Turkish coffee is served with Turkish delight.*

YOGURT DRINK (AYRAN)*

INGREDIENTS

32 oz plain yogurt

2½ c cold water

Salt to taste (~1 tsp)

PREPARATION

Mix ingredients together until well blended.

BLACKBERRY DRINK (BOGURTLEN SERBETI)**

INGREDIENTS

1 lb blackberries (fresh or frozen)

2 c sugar

5-6 c water

3-4 cloves

PREPARATION

Put blackberries in a bowl, add sugar and refrigerate overnight. The next day, boil the blackberries and sugar with the water for 30-40 minutes. Skim the foam that forms on the surface. Add cloves, turn the heat off and let it cool. Remove the cloves before pureeing with a hand blender. Strain the syrup if you prefer it have no pulp. Serve chilled.

BLUEBERRY DRINK (YABAN MERSINI SERBETI)**

INGREDIENTS

11 oz Blueberries

2 cloves

10 c water

1½ c sugar

Juice of 1 lemon

4 lemon wedges

PREPARATION

Boil blueberries, cloves and water for about 40 minutes. When the blueberries soften and lose color, turn the heat off. Strain the mixture, returning the liquid to the pot. Mix in sugar and lemon juice over medium heat, stirring continuously until the sugar melts. Turn off the heat. Pour the syrup into a pitcher. Cool and refrigerate. Serve in a glass with lemon wedges.

CRANBERRY DRINK (KIZILCIK SERBETI)**

INGREDIENTS

1 lb fresh cranberries

8 c water

2 c sugar

½ tsp ground cinnamon (optional)

3 cloves (optional)

PREPARATION

Rinse cranberries and remove any stems. Boil 8 cups of water, add all other ingredients, and stir until sugar melts. Cover and boil over medium heat for 25-30 minutes, stirring occasionally. Strain and serve chilled

TAMARIND DRINK (DEMIRHINDIBAG SERBETI)**

INGREDIENTS

3.2 oz tamarind

8 c water (divided use)

1 sticks cinnamon

3 cloves

1 c sugar

PREPARATION

Wash and soak the tamarind overnight in a pot with 3 cups of water. The next day add 5 more cups of water, cinnamon sticks, and cloves. Bring to a boil over medium heat, lower the heat, and simmer for about an hour. Strain and mix in sugar while the syrup is still hot, stirring until the sugar melts. Serve chilled.

The Story of Tamarind Drink and Sultan Suleyman

It was a very hot summer day. Sultan Suleyman was visiting one of the Janissary corps. He was thirsty and asked for a cold drink. They served ice-cold Tamarind syrup in a bowl, and he liked it so much that he ordered the bowl filled with gold and given to the chef.

NEW MOM DRINK (LOHUSA SERBETI)*

INGREDIENTS

3 c water

1 c sugar

1 cinnamon stick

3 cloves

2-3 drops red food coloring

PREPARATION

Boil sugar, cinnamon stick, and cloves with the water. Add the food coloring and boil for 2 more minutes. Strain and serve warm or chilled.

Note: *In Turkey, when a woman has a baby, neighbors and relatives come to visit her and see the baby. For guests, this new mom syrup is prepared and served. It is believed that this syrup is good for strengthening the immune system and, for the new mother, increasing the supply of breast milk.*

LEMONADE (LIMONATA)**

INGREDIENTS

6 thick-skinned lemons

1½ c + 1 tsp sugar

8 c water

PREPARATION

Juice the lemons and keep the rind. Boil the lemon rinds in enough water to cover them. Mix in 1 cup of sugar and the lemon juice. Refrigerate overnight. The next day, strain the lemonade, squeezing any remaining liquid from the lemon rinds. Add remaining sugar and water and mix until sugar is dissolved.

COMPOTES

FRUIT COMPOTE (TAZE MEYVE KOMPOSTOSU)*

INGREDIENTS

1 c raisins

½ c dried apricots (diced)

7 c water

1½ c sugar

¼ c lemon juice

1 banana

1 kiwi

4-5 strawberries

PREPARATION

Boil raisins and dried apricots in a big pot with the water over medium heat for about 15 minutes. Mix in sugar and lemon juice. Stir continuously until the sugar is melted. Cool and refrigerate. Before serving, chop banana, kiwi and strawberry. Mix the fruits into the chilled compote and serve.

About Compote: *Compote is made by boiling fruit in water with sugar. Actually, when made with dried fruits it is called "Hosaf" in Turkish, whereas compote is made with fresh fruits. Hosaf is derived from "Hos-Ab" which means nice-sweet-water. Compotes are served in bowls as a side to drink with a spoon with pilafs and main dishes.*

APPLE CINNAMON DRINK (ELMALI TARCIN SERBETI)**

INGREDIENTS

4 medium apples

1 stick cinnamon

10 c water

1 tbsp ground cinnamon

1½ c sugar

Juice of 4 lemons

PREPARATION

Wash apples and cut each one into 8 pieces (It is ok to keep the seeds in the apple). Boil apple, cinnamon and water in a big pot for about 45 minutes. When the apples soften, strain the liquid. Mix ground cinnamon, sugar and lemon juice into the liquid and stir until sugar melts. Cool and refrigerate before serving.

RAISIN COMPOTE (UZUM KOMPOSTOSU)*

INGREDIENTS

2 c golden raisins

6 c water

2 tbsp honey

PREPARATION

Boil raisins with water in a pot. When it comes to a boil, lower the heat, covers, and cook for 40 more minutes. Turn the heat off, mix in honey, and cool.

DRIED APRICOT COMPOTE (KURU KAYISI KOMPOSTOSU)**

INGREDIENTS

½ lb dried apricots

6 c water

1 c sugar

PREPARATION

Rinse dried apricots and drain. Boil apricots with water over medium heat. Mix in sugar and stir occasionally to cook for about 15 minutes. Cool and refrigerate. Serve chilled.

The Oil of Compote

Ottoman soldiers in the Janissary corps were served their meals with a special spoon (that has verses and prayers on it). The chef served rice pilaf first and then used the same spoon to serve the compote. Therefore the compote developed some residual oil from the rice pilaf. When the Sultan saw this oily compote, he ordered that the compote should be served first and then the rice pilaf so that the spoon didn't transfer oil from the pilaf to the compote. When the soldiers saw that the compote was different, they started a rebellion thinking that they were now being served something inferior. They started shouting, "We want the oily compote!"

PICKLES

PICKLED CUCUMBERS (SALATALIK TURSUSU)**

INGREDIENTS

1 lb baby cucumbers, (if not available use Persian cucumbers) (washed)

1½ tsp salt

3 cloves of garlic

½ c vinegar

1½ c bottled water

46 oz jar (boiled, sterilized)

PREPARATION

Place cucumbers, salt, garlic, vinegar and water in a jar. Make sure the cucumbers are covered, adding more water if needed. Let the cucumbers sit at room temperature for 4 days. Refrigerate after opening.

PEPPERS WITH OIL (YAGLI BIBER TURSUSU)**

INGREDIENTS

2 tbsp olive oil

1 lb banana peppers (seeded and chopped)

6 cloves garlic (whole)

6 roma tomatoes (chopped or shredded)

½ c apple cider vinegar

Salt to taste

PREPARATION

Put oil in a saucepan and add banana pepper and garlic cloves. Sauté for about 3 minutes. Add tomatoes, vinegar, and salt and sauté until most of the liquid has cooked away. If you want to serve as a dip, stop cooking when the mixture is the desired consistency. Put in a jar and screw on the lid securely. Turn upside down until cool to pressurize. Store jars at room temperature, keep opened jars in the refrigerator.

PICKLED CABBAGE (LAHANA TURSUSU)**

INGREDIENTS

4 c water (to boil the cabbage)

1 head cabbage (2-3 lb) (sliced thinly)

5 c distilled white vinegar

1 tbsp salt

4 c water (boiled and cooled down)

8 cloves garlic (peeled)

¼ c red cabbage (optional)

PREPARATION

Boil 4 cups water in a pot, add the cabbage, turn off the heat and let stand for about 3 minutes. Drain. Mix vinegar, salt and 4 cups boiled and cooled down water until the salt is dissolved. Transfer one fourth of the cabbage to a jar and pour one fourth of the vinegar water mix liquid onto it. Repeat the layering with the rest of the cabbage and liquid. Drop the garlic into the jar. You may put some red cabbage in the third layer if you want pink pickled cabbage. Close the jar lid tightly and leave at room temperature for 3-4 days and your pickled cabbage is ready.

PICKLED RED CABBAGE (KIRMIZI LAHANA TURSUSU)*

INGREDIENTS

1 medium red cabbage (sliced thinly)

1 tsp salt

5 tbsp apple cider vinegar

PREPARATION

Add vinegar and salt to red cabbage and squeeze and crush a few minutes with your hand. Store in an airtight container. Keep refrigerated. Serve chilled.

YOGURT**

INGREDIENTS

4 c whole milk

2 tbsp plain yogurt

Kitchen thermometer

PREPARATION

Boil the milk and let it cool until around 110°F - 113°F (if you do not have a kitchen thermometer, you may use your finger to estimate the temperature. You may test briefly, and if you can hold the tip of your finger in the milk for 7-8 seconds, it means the temperature is right. Be careful not to burn your finger, use a thermometer to be on the safe side). Lay a towel or a piece of cloth on your kitchen counter and place the pot on it. Slowly mix the plain yogurt into the milk then cover. Wrap the pot in 3-4 kitchen towels to enclose it. Let it sit at room temperature 8-10 hours in winter or 6-8 hours in summer. Refrigerate at least one day before serving.

CHEESE CURDS (COKELEK)***

INGREDIENTS

1 gallon whole milk

1¼ c vinegar

PREPARATION

Boil milk and vinegar for 30 minutes until lumps form. Stir it every 10 minutes. These lumps are cheese curds. Drain in a colander lined with cheesecloth, salt the curds, and leave to drain completely, about 2 hours. Transfer to a storage container and refrigerate. Eat within 2 weeks. Cheese curds can be eaten for breakfast or used in salads or pastries.

CREAM CHEESE (KREM PEYNIR)***

INGREDIENTS

1 lb plain yogurt

1 tbsp salt

2 tbsp dill (chopped)

½ tsp black cumin

PREPARATION

Add salt to yogurt and bring to a boil over medium heat stirring occasionally. Set a cheesecloth-lined colander over a bowl and drain the boiled yogurt for several hours at room temperature, reserving the liquid that collects in the bowl. Draw up the sides of the cheesecloth, tying it shut so the yogurt is completely enclosed. Lift the colander and transfer the reserved liquid in the bowl to a saucepan. Bring it to a boil and add the drained yogurt secured tied up in the cheesecloth. Boil for about 15 minutes. Drain again for several hours and spoon out your cheese, mix in dill and black cumin. Store in a container and refrigerate, consuming within a couple of weeks.

JAMS

STRAWBERRY JAM (CILEK RECELI)***

INGREDIENTS

4 c organic strawberries (pick small, red ones)

4 c sugar

Juice of 1 lemon

Jars (boiled, sterilized)

PREPARATION

Remove stems and leaves from the strawberries and wash them. Cut the bigger strawberries into two or three pieces. Put the strawberries in a big pot, add the sugar, and let sit overnight with the lid ajar. In the morning, bring strawberries to a boil, stirring occasionally. Make sure to watch over the pot as it may bubble up very quickly. Reduce heat and keep boiling for about 1 hour. Add lemon juice in the last five minutes. Homemade strawberry jam will be thinner in consistency than store-bought. Store your jam in boiled, sterilized jars. Fill jars and close the lid while the jam is still hot. Cool and refrigerate.

ORANGE PEEL JAM (PORTAKAL KABUGU RECELI)****

INGREDIENTS

Peel of 6 oranges (use 2 oranges to make the orange juice)

Warm water to cover (to be repeated 3 times)

1 c water

⅓ c orange juice

2⅓ c sugar

¼ tsp lemon juice

PREPARATION

Rinse the oranges. Using a knife, cut vertical lines to divide the peel into 8 parts. Peel each slice, removing as much pith as possible from the peel. (Save the fruit itself for eating or juicing.) Make a roll with each peel with your hand and sew and thread into a circle shape (as pictured). Place the peels on the thread in a bowl with warm water to cover for about 1 hour. Change the water and boil for 30 minutes. Replace the water one more time and bring to a boil, boiling for 1 more hour. When the peels are softened and no longer bitter, add the water and the orange juice and bring back to a boil. Stir in the sugar. After about 30 minutes add lemon juice and boil for 1-2 more minutes. Cool, remove the thread from the peels, and pour into a sterile jar. Put the lid on and store refrigerated.

CHERRY JAM (VISNE RECELI)*

INGREDIENTS

15 oz. cherries in heavy syrup (pitted dark sweet)

2½ c sugar

1 tsp lemon juice

PREPARATION

Boil cherries in heavy syrup (pitted dark sweet) with sugar in a pot over medium-low heat for 35 minutes. Stir in lemon juice and boil for 5 more minutes. Cool and pour into a sterile jar. Put the lid on and store refrigerated.

PEACH MARMALADE (SEFTALI MARMELATI)**

INGREDIENTS

2 lb peaches (peeled and diced)

2 c sugar

Juice of half a lemon

3 cloves

PREPARATION

Place peaches and sugar in a pot and let them sit for 5 hours at room temperature. Next boil them until peaches are softened (No need to add additional liquid). Then carefully puree with a stick blender. Add cloves and boil for 30 more minutes. Remove the foam that collects on the surface. Turn the heat off when it reaches a pudding consistency. Pour into sterile jars while still hot, screw lids on securely, and turn upside down to pressurize. Cool, turn upwards and store refrigerated.

DIPS

OLIVE PASTE DIP (ZEYTIN EZMELI SOS)*

INGREDIENTS

1 c olive paste (see note below)

1 tbsp tomato paste

1 tbsp pepper paste

2 garlic cloves (minced)

2 tbsp olive oil

¼ tsp black pepper

¼ tsp red pepper

½ tsp oregano

Salt to taste

PREPARATION

Mix all ingredients and serve with bread.

Olive paste: *Olive paste is made from ground olives. There are a wide range of uses for olive paste, and as a result it is a frequent feature in Mediterranean kitchens. Many delis and markets carry olive paste, and it is also possible to make it at home. Pit black olives using the side of a knife to gently crush the olive and push out the pit. Puree using a stick blender.*

TOMATO PASTE DIP (ACUKA)*

INGREDIENTS

3 tbsp tomato paste

1 tbsp red pepper paste

2 medium tomatoes (grated)

2 tbsp olive oil

¼ tsp black pepper

¼ tsp ground red pepper

¼ tsp fenugreek (optional, see note below)

½ tsp oregano

½ tsp cumin

1 clove garlic (minced)

2 tbsp walnuts (chopped)

PREPARATION

Mix all ingredients and sauté for about 10 minutes. Cool and serve at room temperature. Also, you can serve with bread, crackers, chips and crudités.

Fenugreek: *Cemen, Fenugreek is an herb that comes from the leaves of the fenugreek plant. It has a bitter, spicy taste. Fenugreek is used especially in making pastrami. Some dipping sauces also contain fenugreek as an optional spice.*

HUMMUS (HUMUS)**

INGREDIENTS

1 can garbanzo beans (rinsed and drained)

2 garlic cloves (minced)

Juice of 1 lemon

1 tbsp cumin

Salt to taste

½ c tahini (see note below)

1 tsp sumac

2 tbsp olive oil

PREPARATION

Puree beans with a blender. Add garlic, lemon juice, cumin, salt, and tahini and mix well. Top with sumac and olive oil. Serve with bread or chips.

Tahini: *Tahini is a paste made from ground sesame seeds. It is used as a dip on its own or as a major component of hummus, baba ghanoush, and halva.*

A visit to Samanyolu TV's cooking show, Yeşil Elma, just prior to broadcast. The group received a quick lesson in Turkish cooking from the famous host Oktay Usta.

Raindrop Turkish House

Raindrop Turkish House is a non-profit 501(c)(3), educational, charitable, social and cultural organization founded by Turkish-Americans in Houston in 2000 and now it operates in six states: Texas, Arkansas, Kansas, Oklahoma, Mississippi, and Louisiana.

Next to being a home to Turkish-Americans, Raindrop Turkish House addresses their social and cultural needs and helps them integrate into this multicultural society better. The mission of Raindrop is to introduce Turkish culture into American society and cultivate friendship and promote the understanding of diverse cultures through its unique services to the community, through dialog and cooperation.

Raindrop contributes in colorful life of society by organizing, sponsoring and hosting cultural and social events such as Turkish cuisine classes, cultural nights, Nevruz picnics, traditional dinners, Turkish coffee nights, International Women's day, soccer games, Noah's pudding days, Whirling Dervishes' performances, and Intercultural Dialog Dinners where we enjoy and strengthen friendship ties with our neighbors and local communities and form a culture of "living together." We also host artistic exhibitions throughout the year.

One of the main events that Raindrop Turkish House organizes is the annual Turkish Language and Culture Olympiad. Turkish is one of the critical languages under the National Security Language Initiative (NSLI). NSLI is an interagency initiative of the Departments of State, Education, and Defense, and the Office of the Director of National Intelligence. The initiative is designed to dramatically increase the number of Americans learning critical need foreign languages such as Turkish, Chinese, Persian and others through new and expanded programs from kindergarten throughout university and into the workforce. In order to encourage students to study Turkish and start doing this as early as possible, Raindrop has been organizing Turkish Language and Culture Olympiad with an increasing participation each year.

Raindrop also organizes every year its traditonal Turkic Cultures and Children's Festival where the kaleidoscope of varying people from Turkic World is showcased. Representative bodies and communities from Azerbaijan, Bosnia, Turkey, Turkmenistan, Kazakhstan, The Kyrgyz Republic, Uzbekistan and more celebrate the rich mosaic of variant cultures and heritages with the help of both local and international sponsors. Not only an educational accomplishment for those mesmerized by the amazing sights or for those involved, the Turkic Cultures and Children's Festival is an entertaining event that joins together international communities. This event includes the famous Ottoman Army Band, handcrafts, calligraphy, music groups, folk dances, and of course delicious worldwide known Turkish cuisine.

For the current events and past activities, you can visit the Raindrop website at www.raindropturkevi.org or www.turkishhouse.org

Phone: (713) 974 1412
9301 W. Bellfort Ave.
Houston, TX 77031

INDEX OF RECIPES